A Tale of Two Shamans
Ga Sg̱áagaa Sdáng / Ga Sg̱aaga Sding

Ga Sg̲áagaa Sdáng

Ga Sg̲aaga Sding

Retold and illustrated by
Michael Nicoll Yahgulanaas

A Tale of
Two Shamans

**With parallel texts in the Old Massett, Skidegate and Kaigani (Alaskan)
Dialects of X̱aad Kil / X̱aayda Kil/ X̱aad Kíl, the Haida language**

Locarno Press
VANCOUVER

Notes on A Tale of Two Shamans — Ga SGáagaa Sdáng / Ga SGaaga Sding

The work that you are about to read is old, much older than any of us still living. It is probably older than anything one could even call Canadian. It precedes us all. Obviously I am not the primary creator of such a narrative, but as a Haida citizen, it is an ancestral experience. The strength of owning a thing is often expressed as a right to share it. In this retelling we the illustrators, editors, linguists, curators and indeed the community of living Haidas invite you to join with us. Come as a respected guest. Sit at the table and be nourished by our living culture.

This story is a blend of accounts recorded in the early 1900s in three of the once numerous dialects of the Haida language. This is one of the first publications to include the differing orthography of all three dialects in one edition. In my telling I have blended elements from three separated versions and retold the story, seeking a coherent, unified whole.

The first part of my telling of *Ga SGáagaa Sdáng / Ga SGaaga Sding* comes from Sk'a.aaws. This is an ancient town site located along the eastern border of a forested region called Duu Guusd. Duu Guusd is part of Haida Gwaii, an archipelago once held in its colonial embrace as the Queen Charlotte Islands. The second old source of telling is Skedans. This old town is located in the Gwaii Haanas Haida Heritage site.

The third source text is only a fragment, told and repeated and recorded in the Kaigani dialect from Alaska. In it, one of the shaman brothers is blind, an unseen and unseeing spirit. This twist made the story clearer to me, that it really was about sightedness, our ability to see through things, or not. While this Kaigani record is only a brief fragment, it's a very significant part of understanding this complex story.

In 2001 Haida manga and the Haida Gwaii Museum collaborated to publish a version of an ancient parable that sought to honour all three of the surviving regional dialects, without privileging any dialect over another. There was a need then, as there is now, to construct, maintain and share conversation between the three dialect regions. Today the need ranges from the warmth of kinship, to the somewhat cooler heat of revitalizing National institutions and the decidedly chilly and inevitable international boundary negotiations. The fluent speakers and students of X̱aad Kil/X̱aayda Kil / X̱aad Kíl, my collaborators, have additional and compelling reasons for this 2018 edition. Their scholarly work provides a welcomed and long-awaited precision in phonology, morphology and syntax as understood in the three regions.

My 2001 English language version, which remains unaltered here, is an interpretation of the elements of meaning. The conceptual structure of this parable is about sightedness and the role of transgressions and transitions in a world of symmetry, moieties within the cycle of rebirth. My paintings and text constitute a theory that there is a unified structure of meaning in what was recorded as three separate stories and that these three stories were once a single parable.

Reimagining the common root for these three branches reverses the fracturing of a language that has developed regional distinctions. In addition to the careful structure of language as provided here by Haida scholars, we included the contemporary illustrated and textual voice to question how narratives are more than simple, fixed structures. Parables, histories, narratives, stories and all manners of communication—be they carved, written, spoken or danced—are living instruments recording change and the vibrancy of expression in human societies. What is real in one particular time must be made real, useful and appropriate in another time. This is the ritual of renewal.

Be cautioned that these images are interpretations informed by my own cultural composition and life experiences. This is a contemporary rendering of a worldview first expressed in different times and probably for different reasons. I am not stepping forward to join that dais filled with authorities claiming to represent those distant times. I am a Haida whose life experiences are probably very similar to your own. In many respects that greater distance between the first tellers of *Ga SGáagaa Sdáng / Ga SGaaga Sding* and ourselves makes us both readers.

I have restrained from writing an extensive opinion, instead limiting my retelling to a brief text and illustrations. This should suffice to give the engaged reader a hint of the amazing concepts which ripple through this shamanic tale and remain a substantial element of that dynamic living society of indigenous peoples called Haida.

Michael Nicoll Yahgulanaas

To all the students of this generation who have committed themselves to language revitalization

Once upon a time, this was a
true story....

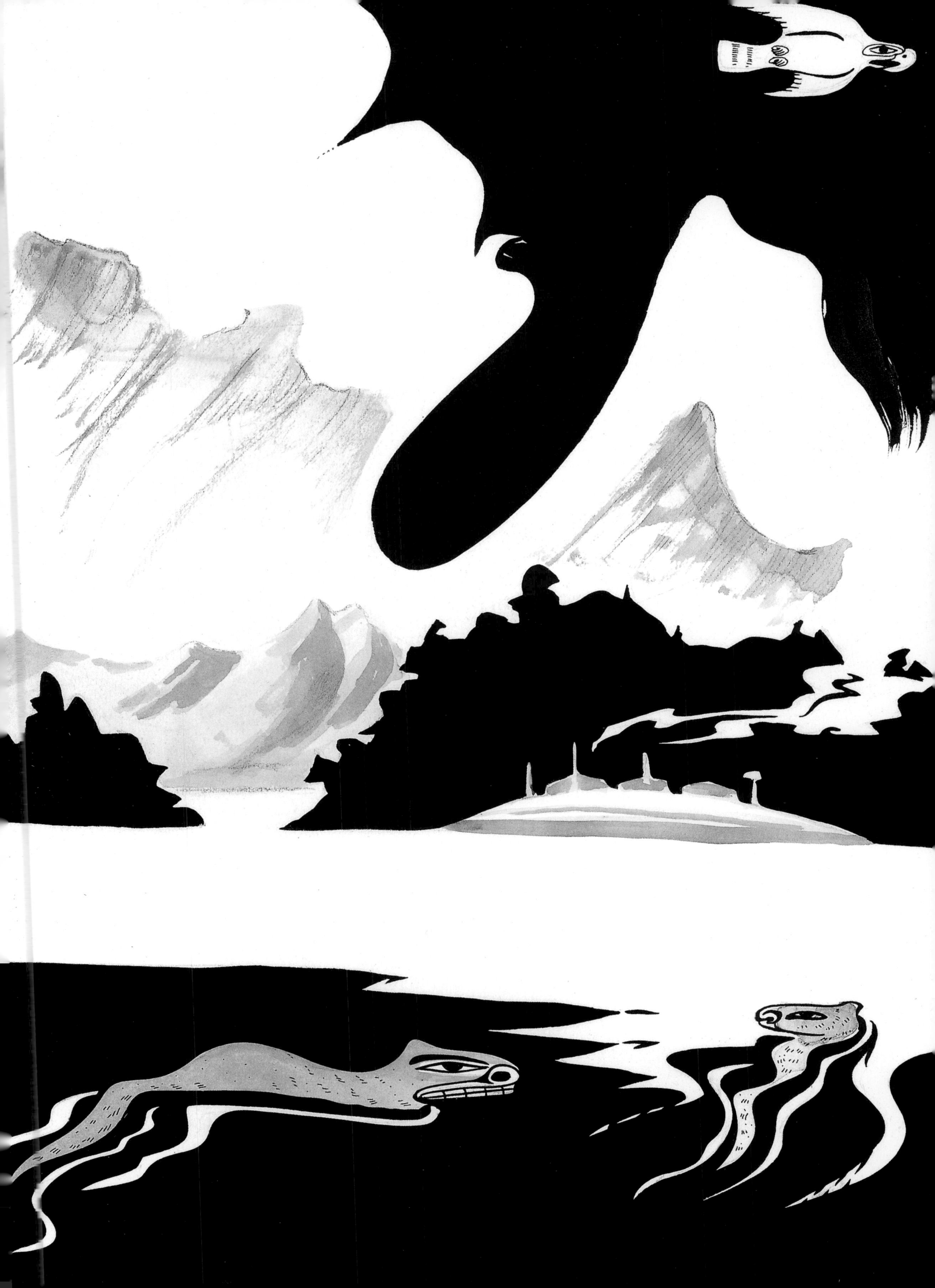

There was a shaman and his partner,
Elder, who loved each other very much.
They lived in Sk'a.aaws town.

"Let's leave this place," the shaman said.

Then they left in separate canoes.

OLD MASSETT (OM): Sk'a.aaws 'laangee gu nang sGaagaa
sdaagulaadaayaan.

Gud 'ahl 'la naang'aawaan gu la kuyaada 'iiwaan'aaw.aan.

"T'll kasaats'an" 'waagyaan hin sdaaguhl'aang 'la suudaayaan.

"Gitlaan.gu?" hin 'laa 'la suudaa.yaan.

"HlGaawt'a kunnGaa'aa" hin 'laa 'la suudaayaan.

'Waagyaan 'la kasaa'aaw.aan.

'Waagyaan nang sGwaan 'laa kunaasda'gan tluu kaaydaan.

SKIDEGATE (S): Sk'aa.aaws Llnagaay guu nang sGaaga
hltaaxwii daaGa gan.

Gud ad 'la naa.uu gan. Daanxan gud ad ll k'uuga Guu gan.

"Hala t'alang kaydts'ang",
'wagen han hltaaxwii 'la suuda gan.

"Giidsgwii?", 'la 'la suuda gan.

"HlGaawt'a Kun", 'la 'la suuda gan.

'Wagen tl'l kaaydan.

'Wagen nang sGaaga aadagas 'la kunGasda tluu kayd gan.

KAIGANI (K): Sk'a'áaws 'lan-gáaygw nang sGáagaa sdáagulaadaayaan.

Gud eehl 'll na'áangaawaan, gu 'll kuyáadä í'waanaawaan.

"Tl'áng kasaa ts'an"
'wáagyaan hín sdáaguhl'aang 'll súudaayaan.

"Tl'áan-g uu?" hín 'láa 'll súudaayaan.

"HlGáawt'a kún aa" hín 'láa 'll súudaayaan.

'Wáagyaan 'll kasaa'áawaan.

'Wáagyaan nang sGwáan 'láa kunáasdä hán tlúu káaydaan.

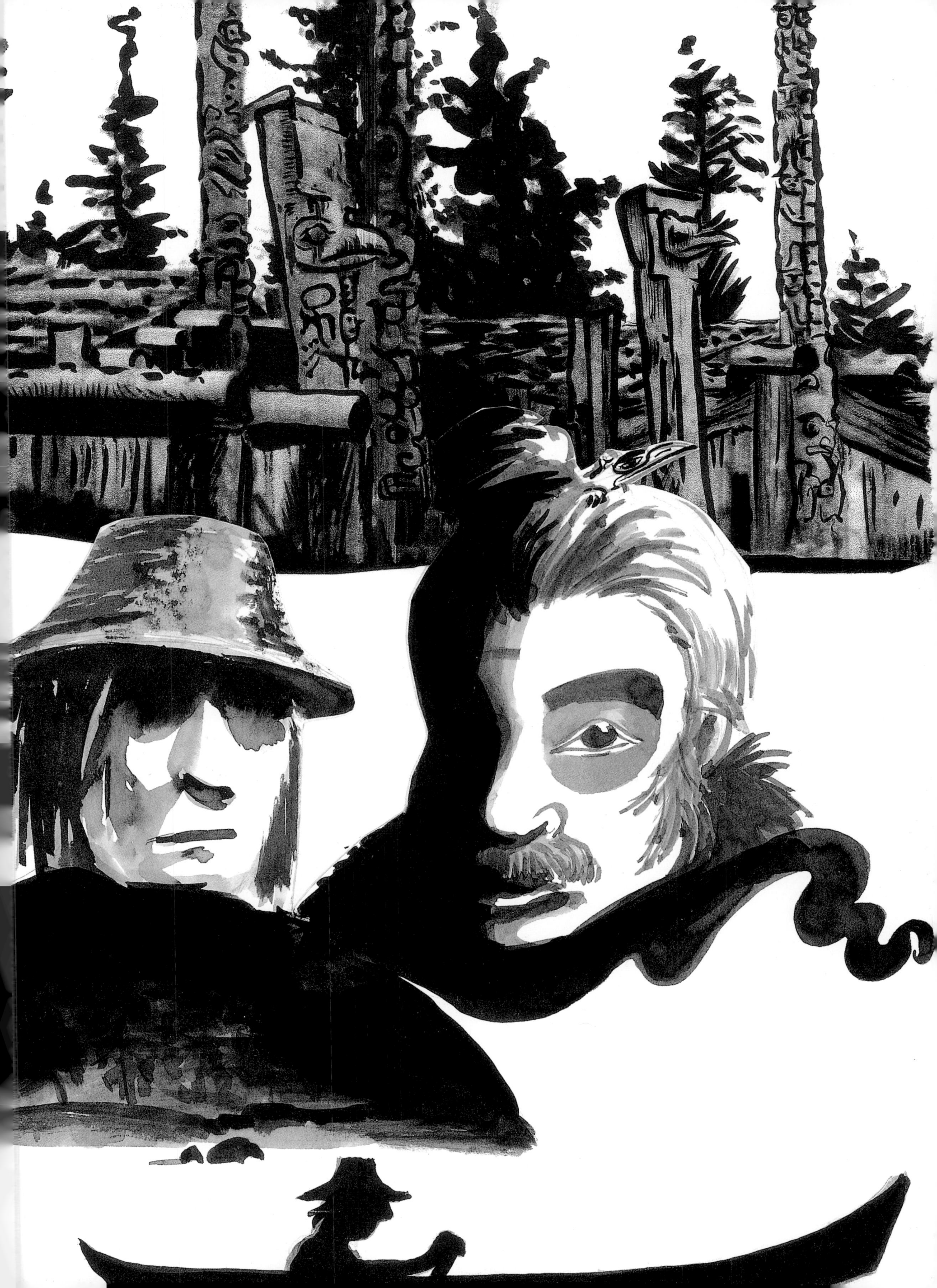

OM: 'Waadluu sdlagu dlagandaal 'la ꞵeengaan.
'Waagyaan 'laa 'la kid.aan.
'Waagyaan 'laa 'la tiyaa.yaan.

Elder saw a river otter swimming along,
and speared it.
They say he killed it.

S: Gen sdllguu dllgingdal 'la ꞵing gan.
'Wagen uu 'la kid gan.
Uu 'la 'la tyah gan.

K: 'Wáadluu sdlagw dlagándaal 'll ꞵéengaan.
'Wáagyaan 'láa 'll kidáan.
'Wáagyaan 'láa 'll tiyáayaan.

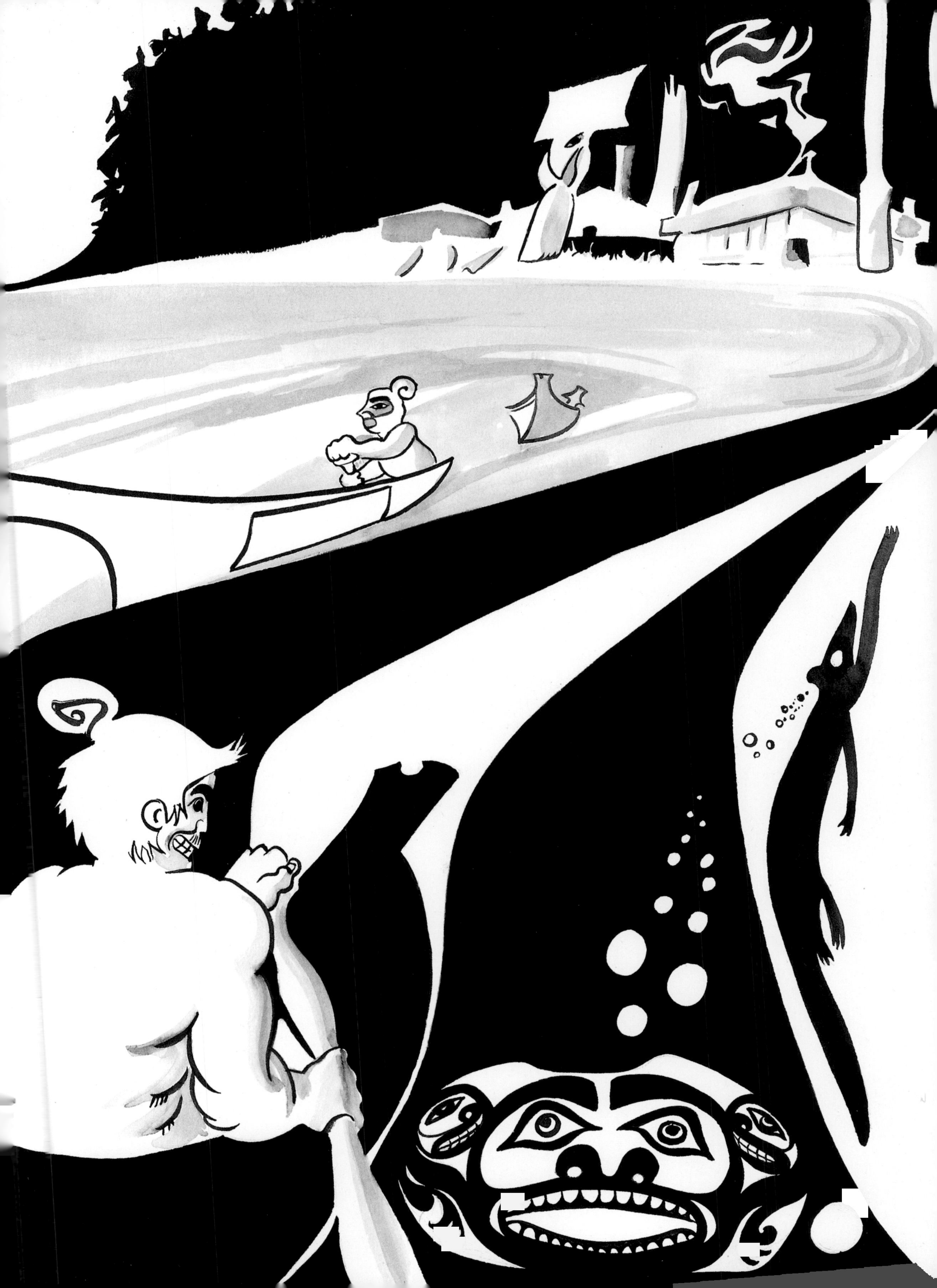

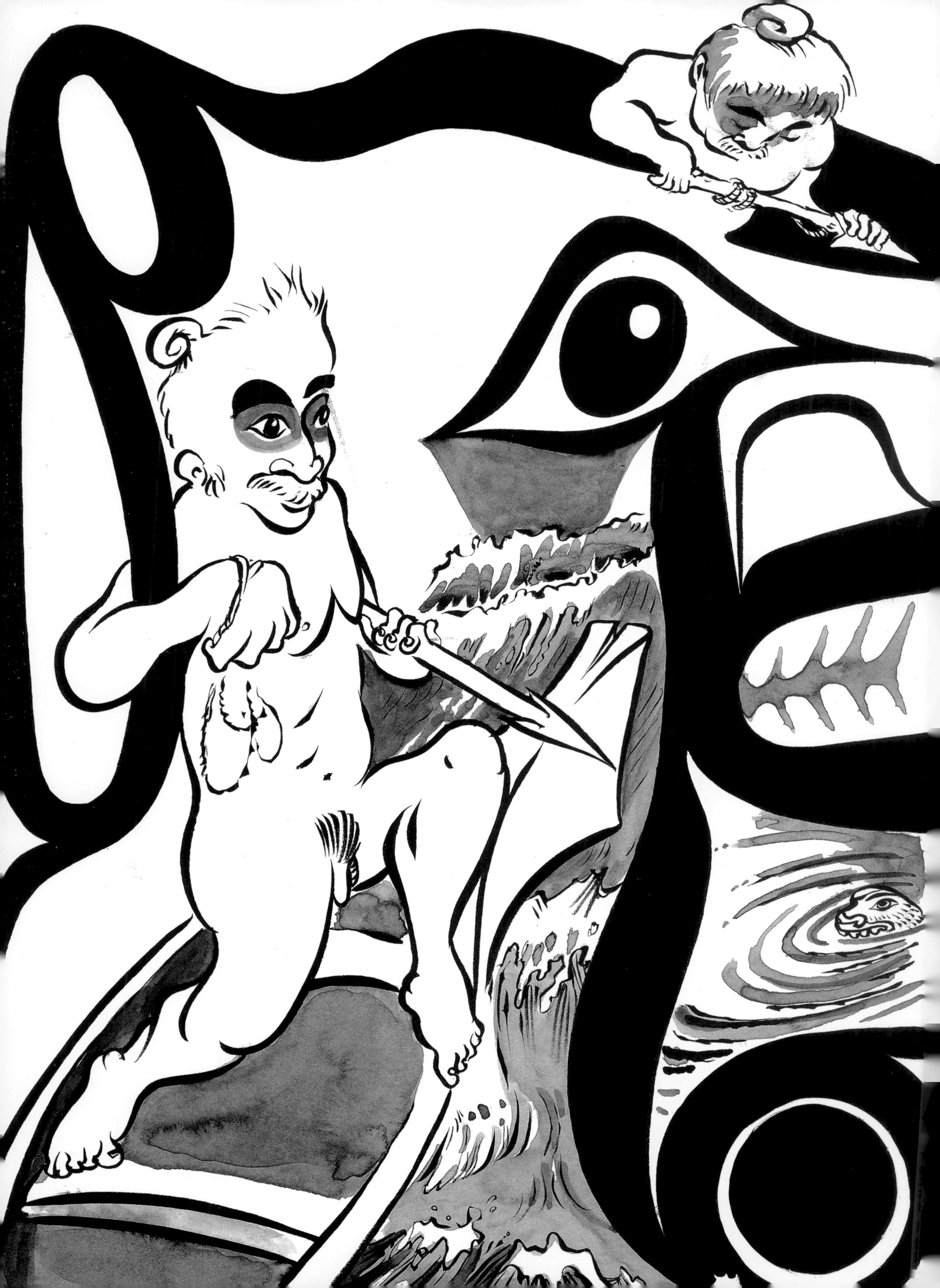

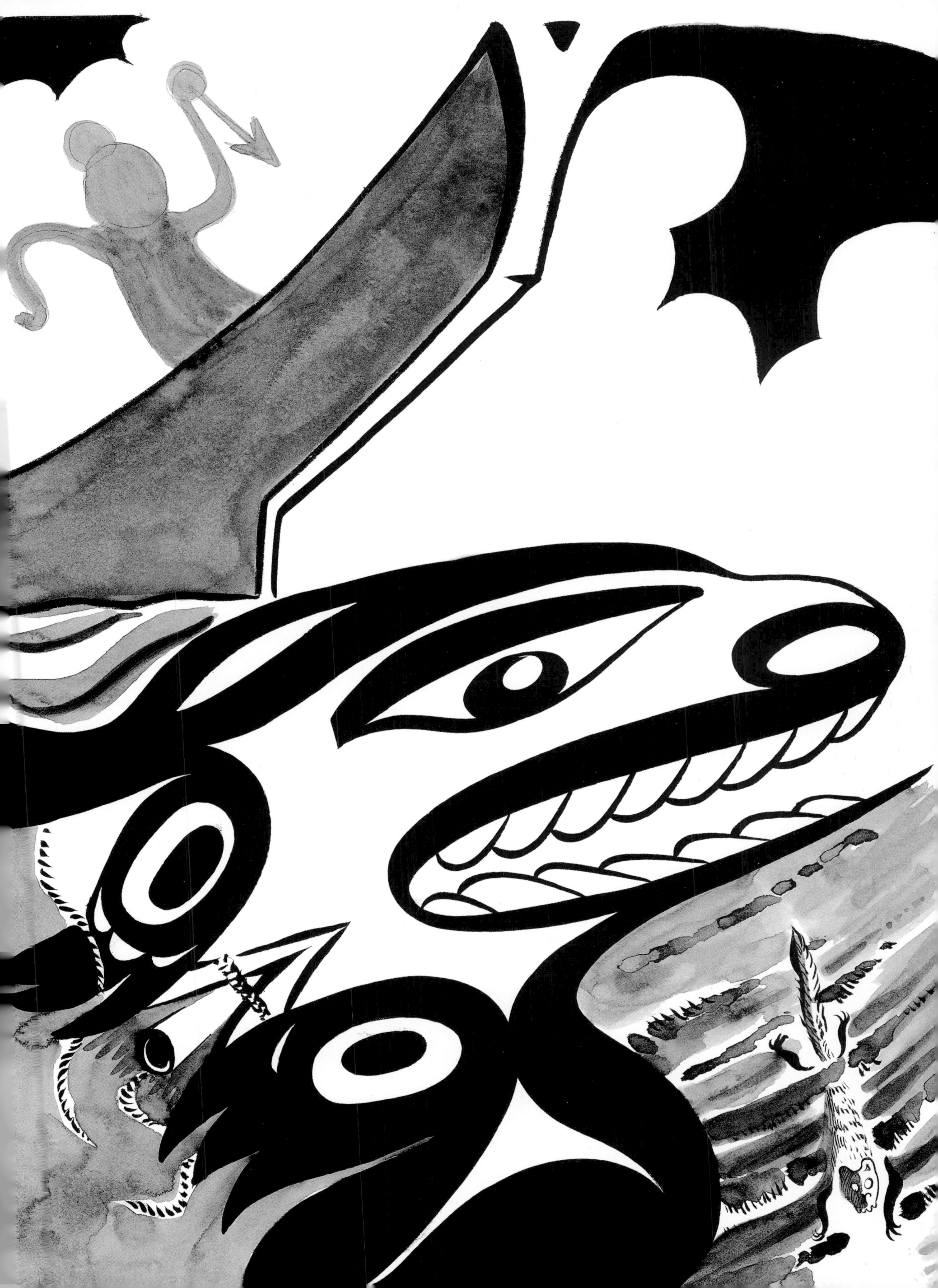

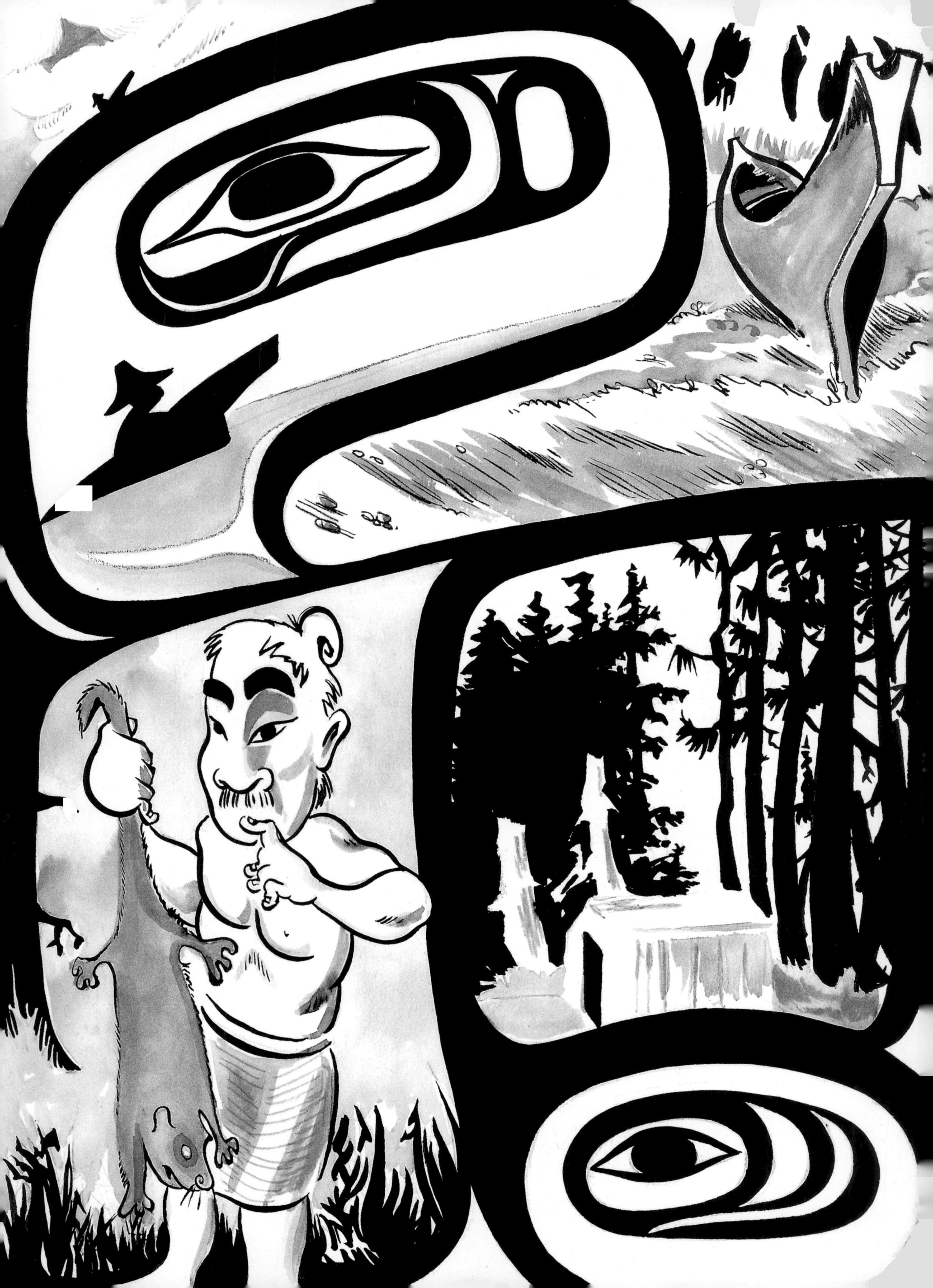

OM: 'Waagyaan hit'an gyaa.aa 'la ts'adaal.'aawaan gu 'la Ga̱sgad.aan.

'Waadluu tl'aa.uu 'la sdaaguhł 'laa dla.a tluu k̲aatl'aa.gaan.

'Waadluu sdlagwee 'la tiyaa.sii 'laa 'la k̲eeng.aan.

"Sdaaguhl, daa.gu sdlagu tiyaa-'ujaa?"

Hin 'laa 'la suudaayaan.

" 'Aang." hin 'la saawaan.

'Waadluu nee 'angaa 'la tlaawhł'agaangaan.

'Waagyaan 'laa G̲iiyhlgii'aawaan. 'waadluu tl'a hit'an 'la ts'aanuu'aawaan.

S: Gaguu 'la ts'iiG̲a xidyas guu 'la kunts'iigil.

Ll hltaaxwii asing 'la sihlG̲a kunts'iigil.

Gen sdllguu 'la tyah gan 'la k̲ing gan.

"Jah, hltaaxwii, sdllguu da tyah gan?"

'La 'la suuda gan.

"Aa.nga." 'La suu gan.

'Wagen naa k'adjuu guu ang.G̲a tl'l hlG̲ang.gul̲xa gan.

Uu G̲iihlgii gan. Naa k'adjuu G̲a tl'l ts'aan.naaw.uuda gan.

K: 'Wáagyaan hat'án gyáa aa 'll ts'adáalaawaan-gw 'll G̲asgadáan.

'Wáadluu tl'aa uu 'll sdáaguhl 'láa dlaa tlúu k̲áatl'aagaan.

'Wáadluu sdlagwáay 'll tiyáasii 'láa 'll k̲éengaan.

"Sdáaguhl, dáa gw sdlagw tiyáa'ujaa?"

hín 'láa 'll súudaayaan.

"Áang," hín 'll sáawaan.

'Wáadluu náay áangaa 'll tlaawhláagaangaan.

'Wáagyaan 'láa G̲íihlgii'aawaan. 'Wáadluu tl'aa hat'án 'll ts'áanuu'aawaan.

Elder came to the place
they were moving to,
where they would build their
house together.

When it was finished, they
made a fire inside.

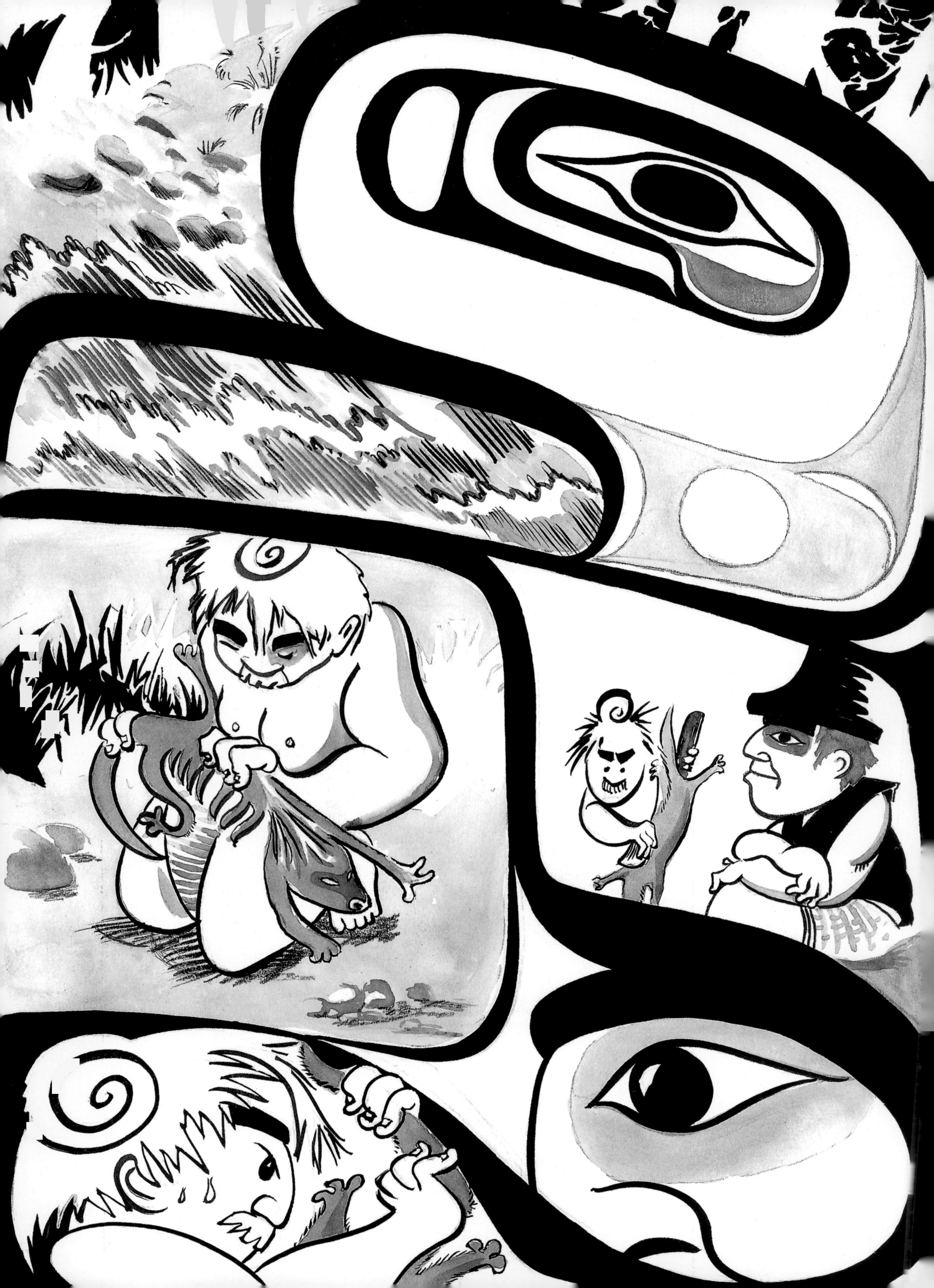

OM: Tl'a hldanuugii sda sdlaguuwee 'angaa 'la tl'ast'aayaan
'waagyaan ts'uu Giiy 'laa 'la da tl'ahlaa.yaan
'la sdaaguhl 'ahl 'laa gudangee 'laa 'iiwaan.aan.
'Waagyaan 'laa xilgaahlaanii.
'Waagyaan hit'an ts'uwee 'waasda 'la dang tl'ast'aayaanii.
'Anaa sangyaas dluu 'la 'waagaan,
'waadluu hi'tan 'la Gaw tla.algwii tla Geelgeeda
'laa 'la gudaangaan
'laa la stl'a sk'adas sandliidaan Gaduu
'la gisgaasii 'la sdaaguhl laa king.gaang.aan.
"Guus gan.uu 'laa dang 'isdaa.asaa'uujang?" Hin 'laa 'la suudaayaan.
"Sgidaan.uu k'aaa Ganaa," hin 'la saawaan.
"Sdaaguhl, hahlgwii hl 'angaa 'isdaa."
Gaduu 'la gisgaasii'ahl.uu 'laa 'la suudaayaan.
'Waagyaan 'laa ga 'laa 'la tl'asdlat'ajaan.

S: Tl'l ga taa Giihlgii gaaydluu, sdllguuwaay 'la tl'lsda gan.
Ts'uu tl'aahlda uu kaahlii Gii 'la giits'ii gan.
Ll hltaaxwii sdllguuwaay k'al ad xang.ahl Gudsdll gan.
Gen 'laa.a sdllguuwaay k'al k'aaGasdll gan.
'Wagen tl'aahldaGaay 'la dansda gan.
Ah naa singxyas dluu 'la 'wáagan.
Gen 'láa Gaw k'yahgwii tl'a daa isjuuGalang
'la 'la guudang gan.
'La 'la Gaaduu stl'lsk'aadas kunsda t'aajing xidii.
Ll hltaaxwii 'la Gan k'aahll kiixa 'la jiigiiGa gan.
"Guus gii.uu da tllGuhlGa guudang?", 'la 'la suuda gan.
"Sk'aang.uu sgiidang.uu k'al Gan ah", ll suu gan.
"Hltaaxwii, dang Ga sdllguu k'al aan gii isda."
Gam uu 'la tllGuhlGa hll.nga Gang, gaayGaagan.ah.
Guuxagang.ngaay sahgud 'la gii 'láa isda.

K: Tl'áa hldanáawgiisdä sdlagwáay áangaa 'll tl'ast'áayaan.
'Wáagyaan ts'úu Gíi 'láa 'll da tl'ahláayaan.
'Ll sdáaguhl Gahl 'láa gudangáay 'láa í'waanaan.
'Wáagyaan 'láa xílgaalaan ii.
'Wáagyaan hat'án ts'uwáay 'wáasdä 'll dáng tl'ast'áayaanii.
Anáa sángyaas dluu 'll 'wáagaan.
'Wáadluu hat'án 'll Gáw tl'a'álgwii tla Géelgeedä 'láa 'll gudáangaan.
'Láa 'll stl'a sk'adas sánsdlhiidaan.
Gadúu 'll jagíiyaasii 'll sdáaguhl 'láa kínggaangaan.
"Gúus Gán uu 'láa dáng isdáasaa'uujang?" hín 'láa 'll súudaayaan.
"Sgidáangw k'áal an aa," hín 'll sáawaan.
"Sdáaguhl, hahlgwíi hl áangaa isdáa."
Gaduu 'll jagíiyaasii eehl uu 'láa 'll súudaayaan.
'Wáagyaan 'láagä 'láa 'll tl'asdlat'ajáan.

That night, after they had eaten,
Elder began to skin the otter.

The shaman noticed that
Elder was unable to properly prepare
the otter's hide.

"Give me the skin," he said.

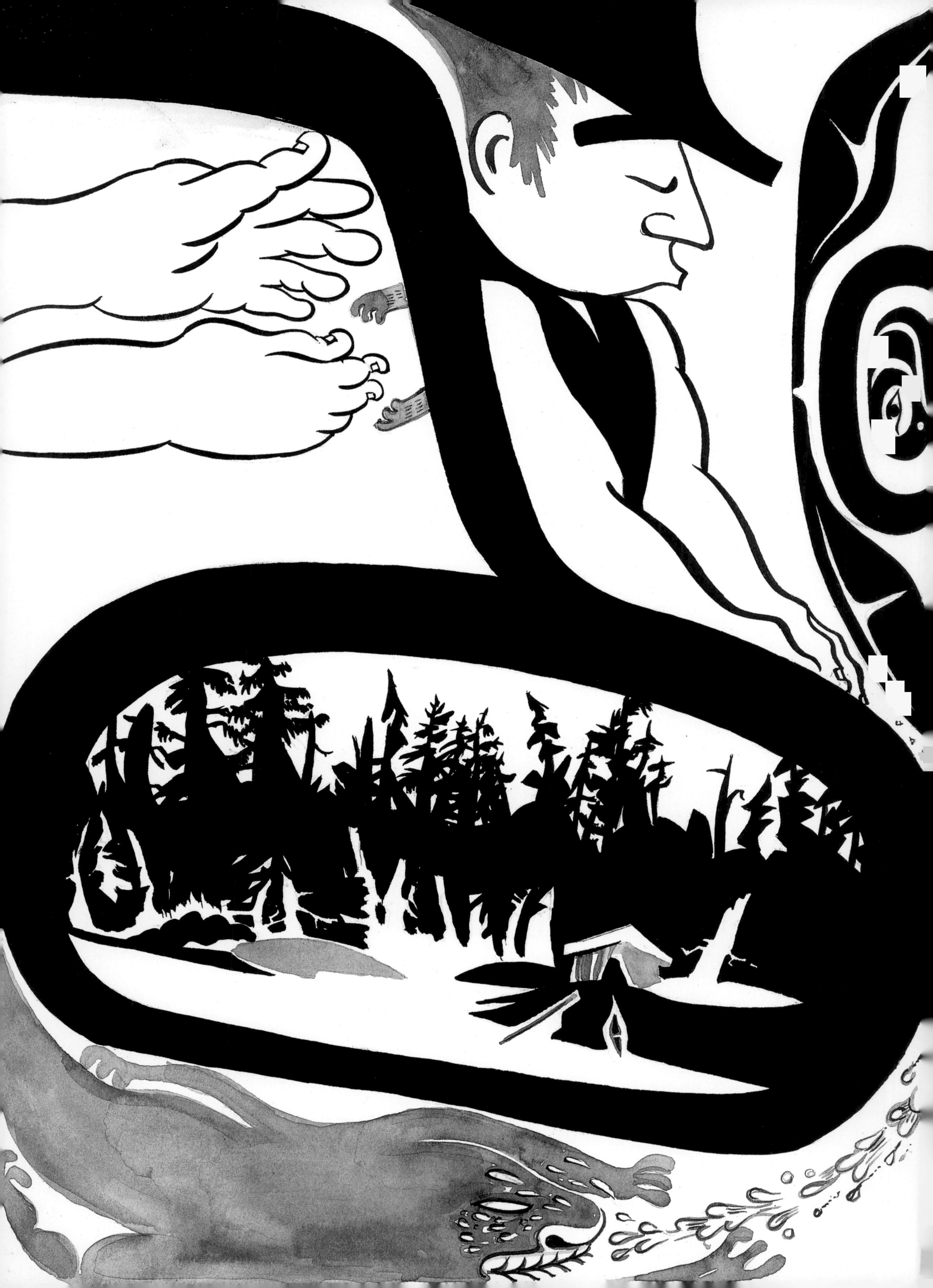

OM: Waagyaan 'laa 'la tl'iids gyaan didgwii dang.ahl 'la xang.aawaan.
Gam 'laa 'la stl'a sk'adas'aan.aan 'laa 'la ging ḵuunaang.aan.
Hing.aan.uu ǥiiy 'laa 'la tsiigaang.aanii.

S: Gam nang sǥaaga uu isxid gen tl'ljuuwaay gwii 'la xang.guu.
Gam 'la stl'lsk'aadas ǥang. 'La 'la ging ḵuunang gan.
Gen ḵ'al ǥii 'la jidsgasda gan.

K: 'Wáagyaan 'láa 'll tl'iids gyáan didgwíi dángahl 'll xangáawaan.
Gám 'láa 'll stl'a sk'adas'áangaan. 'Láa 'll gíng ḵúunaangaan.
Hingáan uu ǥíi 'láa 'll chíigaangaanii.

The shaman took the skin, and turned towards the wall.
He didn't properly prepare the skin; instead, he urinated on it.

21

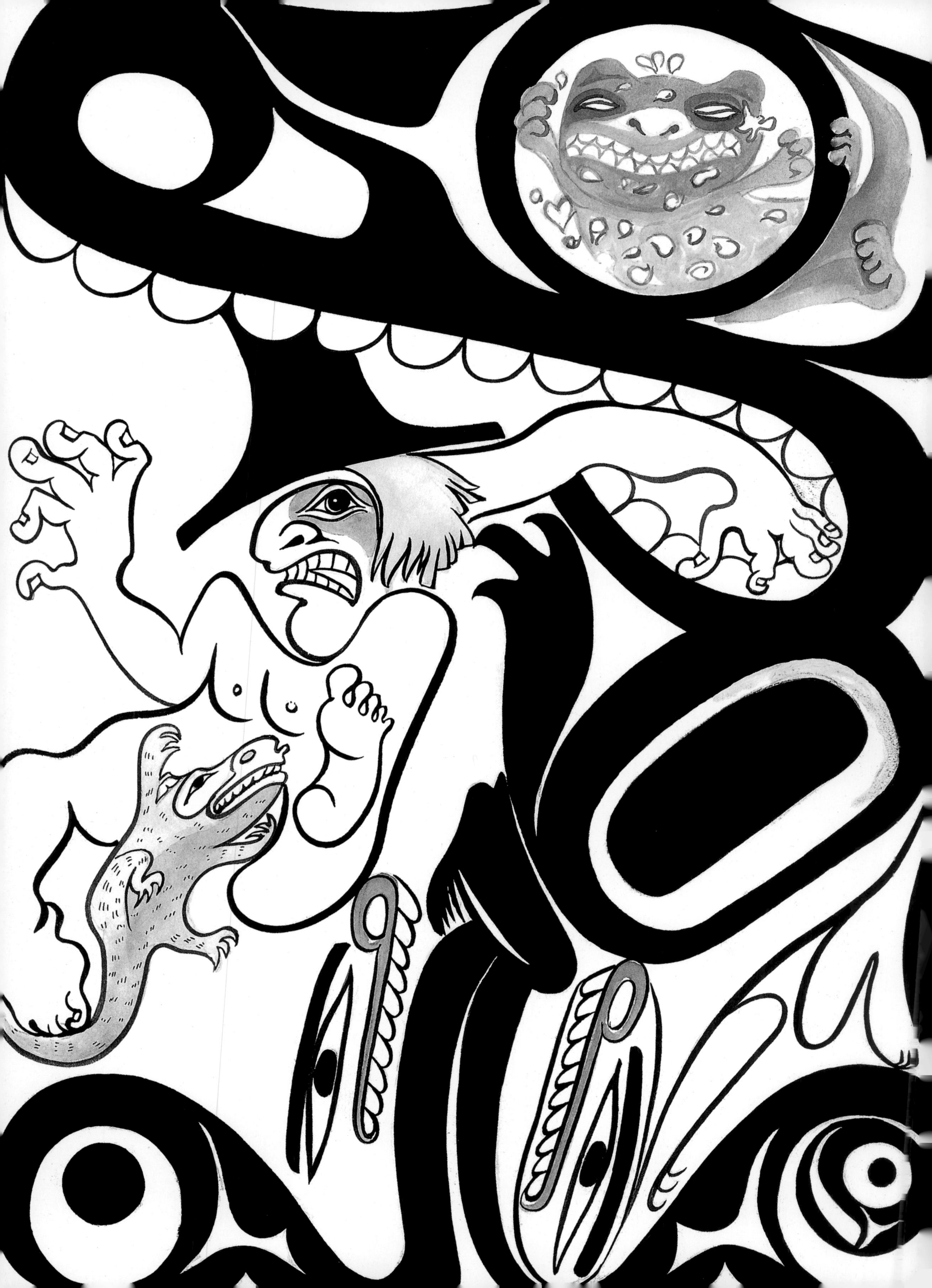

OM: Sdlagwee k̲'al 'la kaahlii.ii k̲ahlaasii
gam G̲an 'la 'unsad'aangaan.
K̲'al 'laa ga 'la tl'asdlat'asii k̲aahliyaan 'la dal 'laa gwaagaalaan.

S: Sdllguu k̲'al G̲aahlandaay ll k̲aahlii G̲ii is hll gan,
gam G̲an ll unsid G̲ang gan.
K̲'al sihlgyang 'la gii 'láa isdayáay dluu ll dal st'ii gil gan

K: Sdlagwáay k̲'ál 'll k̲áahlii ii k̲ahlaasii
gám G̲an 'll únsadaangaan.
K̲'ál 'láag 'll tl'asdlat'asii k̲áahliyaan 'll dál 'láa G̲wáagaalaan.

As soon as the shaman passed the skin
back to Elder, he felt the otter's spirit
in his insides.

Then the shaman's belly began to ache.

23

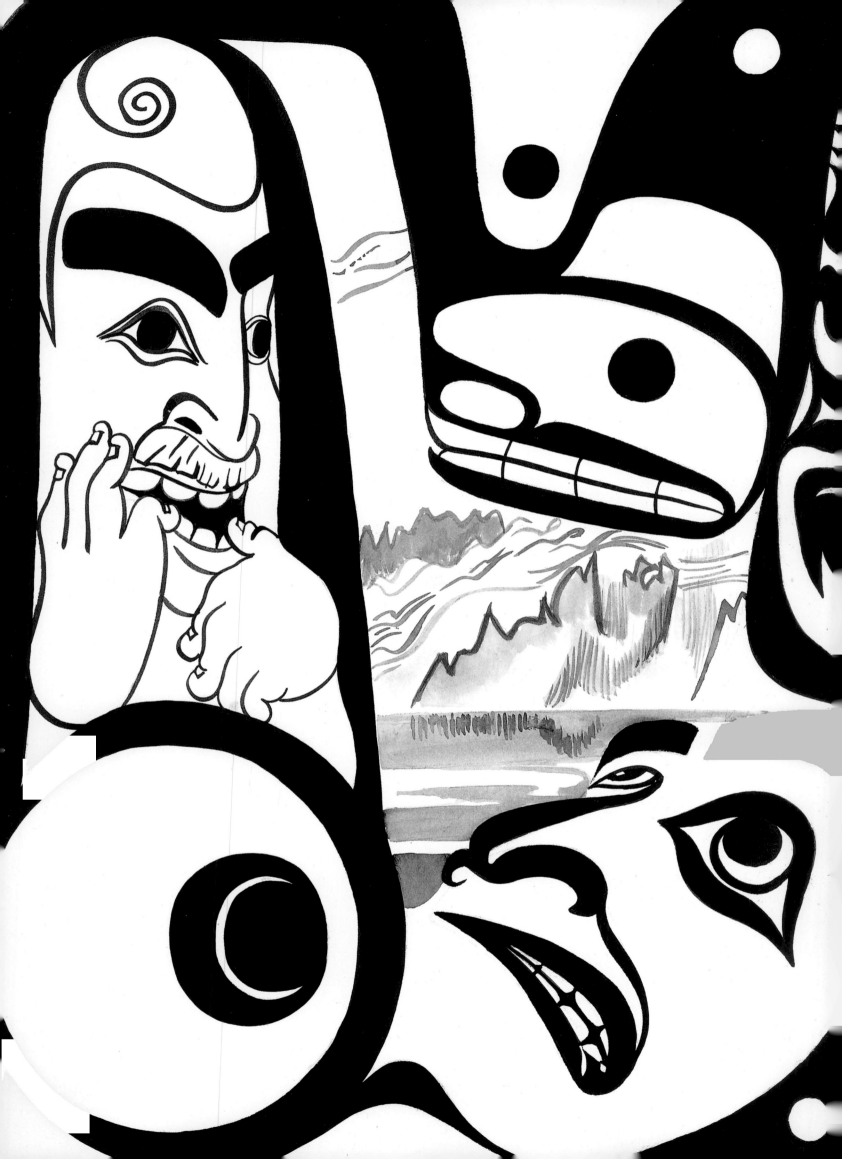

OM: "Sdlagwee dii ahl dang ginang.ganii Ḡahl.uu dang 'iijang.gwaa,"
hin 'laa 'la suudaayaan.

"Yaan.uu dang suugang.gwaa," hin 'laa 'la suudaayaan.

Ḡaal hlḠun.ahlgandaan 'la k'ut'aalaan.

S: Sdllguuwaay dii ad 'la kyaanang gaayḠaagan.uu dang gii gina aahljuu,
'la 'la suuda gan.

"Yahk'ii da suu," 'la 'la suuda gan.

Sing hlḠunuhl gam ll st'ii Ḡang, iilaaw ll k'uud.uul gan.

K: "Sdlagwáay díi eehl dáng ginángganii Ḡahl uu dáng íijanggwaa," hín
'láa 'll súudaayaan.

Yáangk'yaan uu dáng súuganggwaa," hín 'láa 'll súudaayaan.

Ḡáal hlḠúnahlgan dáan 'll k'ut'áalaan.

"That is happening to you because you
asked me for the otter," Elder cried.

"You speak the truth," the shaman
replied.

And in three days, he died.

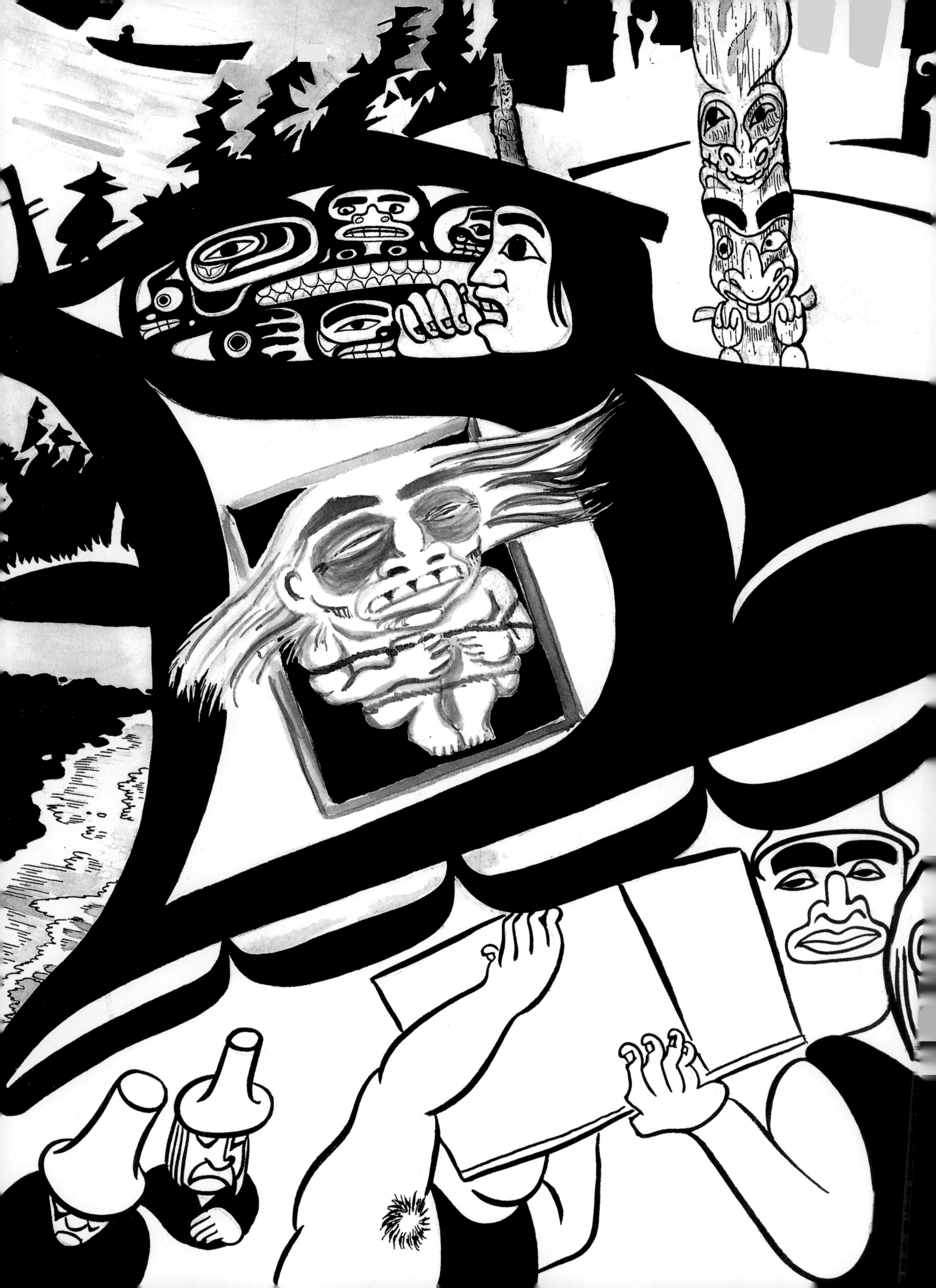

OM: 'Waadluu 'la sdaaguhl sGayhla 'iiwaangaang.aan.
'Waadluu ts'uu 'laa.an tl'a sgi xatl'aayaan.
"Kunngwaa hl 'aajii 'laa k'yuu saa tl'aawhlaaw," hin tl'a saawaan.
'La sdaaguhl.uu suugaan.aan. 'waa gingaan hit'an tl'a 'waagaan.

S: Gen ll hltaaxwii sGaayhll tlaats'iiga gang giinii.
Gen ts'uu 'laa Gan tl'l sgidxuunang gan.
" 'Laa Gan kunjuuwaay guu hlGiiGwa daanaay guu
gina tl'l tllGuhlGa," nang suu gan.
Ll hltaaxwii huu suu gan. 'Wagen haak'wan tl'l 'wáa gan.

K: 'Wáadluu 'll sdáaguhl sGáyhlä í'waan-gaangaan.
'Wáadluu ts'úu 'láa an tl'ä sgi xatl'áayaan.
"Kún-gwaa hl áajii 'láa k'yuu sáa tl'aawhláa'uu," hín tl' sáawaan.
'Ll sdáaguhl uu súugaangaan. 'Wáa gingáan hat'án tl'ä 'wáagaan.

Elder cried hard,

"Build a burial for him on that point."

The people chopped off pieces of cedar.

27

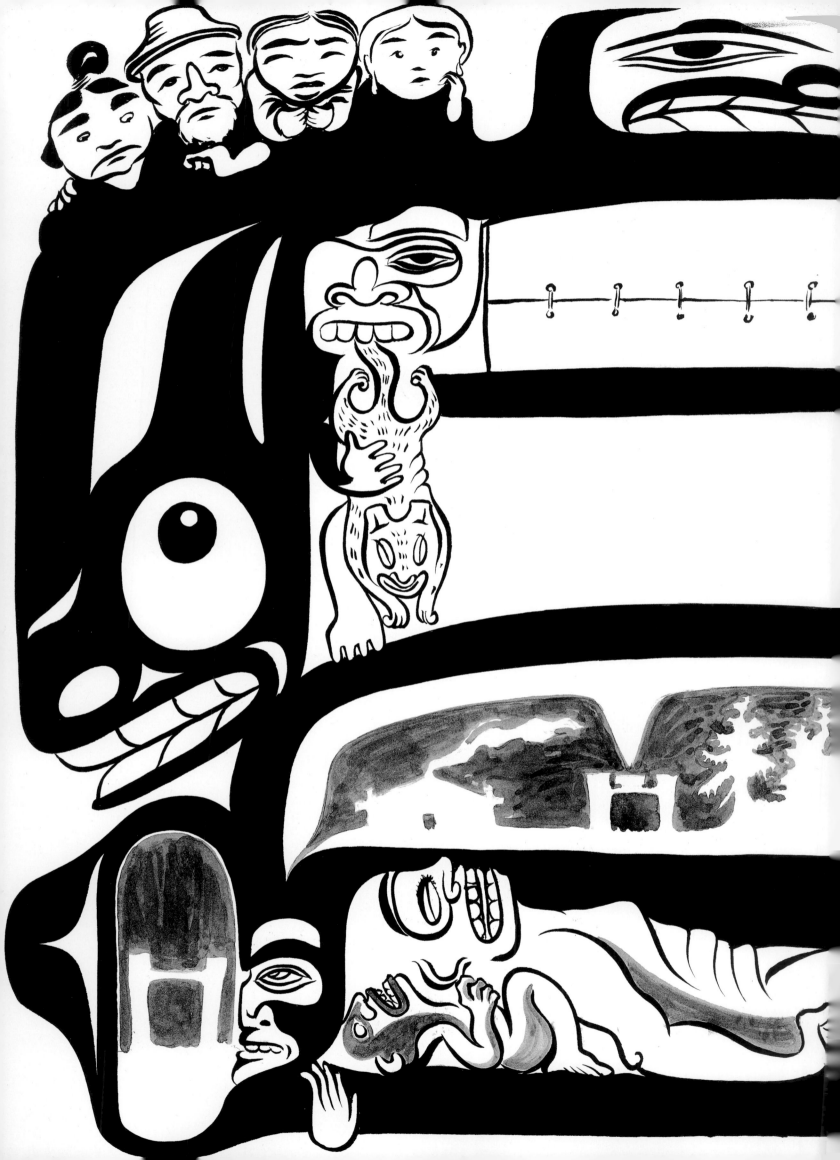

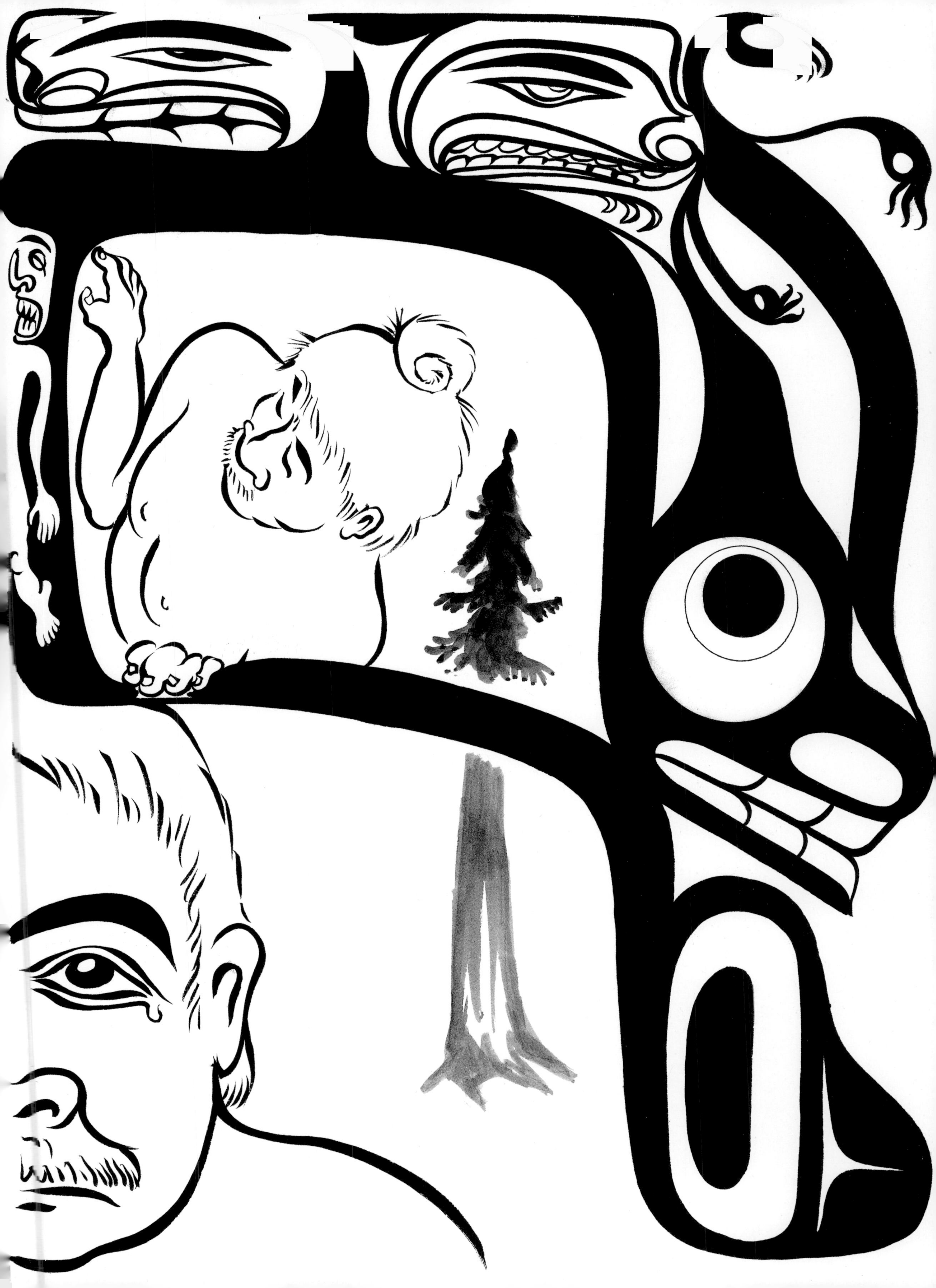

All the time, Elder stayed
near the grave.
He cried.
He blamed himself.

“Why did he ask me for that skin?”

OM: ’Waak’yaahl ’la sdaaguhl sG̱ayhlgaan.aan.
’Waadluu hit’an G̱aa ’laa tl’a ’isdaayaanii, G̱iiyhlgii sdluu aa.
Tlii.uu tlagee sda saa ’iijaanii.
’Waagyaan ’ing.gu hit’an ’laa tl’a dlahlanaagaan.
Waadluu tl’aa.uu ’aajii ’un tl’a tla sk’uuhlgaal.aanii.
“Dii k’ut’ahlsdluu hin dii ḵajaada’waang,” hin ’la saawaan.
’Waagingaan hin ’laa tl’a ḵajaadaayaan.
’La sdaaguhl ’laa ḵ’uhl naagaangaan.
’Laa.aa ’la ḵaa.ayd ’sgyaan ’aajii ’laangaa k’uj’waas hlG̱idga’ la
dlagad’waa sgyaan ’la sG̱ayhlagiigaang.aan.
“Guusgan.uu sdlagwee dii ahl ’la ginaang.aahang.gwaa?”
Hin ’la suugaaan.aan.
’La sG̱ayla.giisgyaan ’la ḵa.aayd.aan. ’Waagyaan ’la jaa taaw
’laa.an tlaawhlgaan.aan.
’Waa daaliig.uu hawisan ’laa.aa ’la ḵaa.aydaan.aan.
’Waadluu hawisan gu ’la sgayhlagaang.aan.
’Waak’yaahl ’laa ’la kunaada.gaang.aan. “Guusgan.uu sdlagwee dii ahl ’la ginaang.
Aa hang.gwaa?” hin ’la suugaang.aan.
’La sG̱ahlagii sda gu ’la ḵaw.a’wagaang.aan.

S: ’Wagen ll hltaaxwii sG̱aayhll gíi gan.
Gen hlG̱iiG̱wa daanaay guu gina ’laa G̱an
tl’l tllG̱uhlG̱a gan, G̱iihlgii gaaydluu G̱ii ’la tl’l isda gan.
Sah G̱aagwii uu is gan tllgaay sdaa.uu.
’Wagen sah gina G̱aahlins guu ’la tl’l isda gan.
Gen G̱aahlins sah guu G̱andlls sda naa uuna tl’l tllG̱uhlG̱a gan.
“Dii taayG̱a gen, dii ḵaajii aan gwii isda,” ll suu gan.
Gen ll ḵaajii gagwii ll kilG̱uhlG̱a gan, G̱aaw tl’l isda gan.
Ll hltaaxwii ’la ḵ’uhlG̱a naa.uu gan.
’Laa gwii ’la is, ll daagul gii ’la ḵ’aw.uu ll ḵanhlln,
gen ll sG̱aayhll gan.
“Gaayintl’aaw dii ad sdllguuwaay gii ’la kyaanang,”
ll suu gan.
Tlaan ll sG̱aayhll gan, gen ll ḵaaydan.
Ll jaaG̱a ’laa G̱an ga taa tllG̱uhlG̱a gang giinii.
DaaG̱alaayG̱a ising ’la gwii ’la sdiihl gan, kunG̱asda gaa.ngang.
Gen ll sG̱aayhll gan, kunG̱asda gaa.ngang.
Agan ’la kuunada gii.
“Gaayintl’aaw dii ad sdllguuwaay gii ’la kyaanang?”,
ll suu gan.
Ll sG̱aayhll gan sdaa.uu, ll ḵ’aw.uu dii gan.

K: ’Wáa k’yáahlg ’ll sdáaguhl sG̱áyhlgaangaan.
’Wáadluu hat’án G̱áa ’láa tl’ä isdáayaan ii, G̱íihlgiis dluu aa.
Tlíi uu tlagáaysdä sáa ijáanii.
’Wáagyaan ínggw hat’án ’láa tl’ä dlahlanáagaan.
’Wáadluu tl’aa uu áajii ún tl’ä tla sk’úuhlgaalaanii.
“Díi k’ut’ahls dluu hín díi kajaadä’waang,” hín ’ll sáawaan.
’Wáa gingáan hín ’láa tl’ ḵajáadaayaan.
’Ll sdáaguhl ’láa k’uhl náagaangaan.
’Láa aa ’ll ḵáayds gyáan áajii ’láangaa k’uj’wáas hlG̱idgä ’ll
dlagad’wáas gyáan ’ll sG̱áyhlägiigaangaan.
“Gúus gán uu sdlagwáay díi eehl ’ll gináangaa, hánggwaa?”
hín ’ll súugaaanaan.
’Ll sG̱áylägiis gyáan ’ll ḵáaydaan.
’Wáagyaan ’ll jáa táaw ’láa an tlaawhlgáanaan.
’Wáa daalíigw háwsan ’láa aa ’ll ḵáaydaanaan.
’Wáadluu háwsan gu ’ll sG̱áyhlägaangaan.
’Wáa k’yáahlg ’láa ’ll kunáadägaangaan. “Gúus gán uu sdlagwáay díi eehl ’ll
ginaangaa hang gwaa?” hín ’ll súugaangaan.
’Ll sG̱áyhlägiisdä gu ’ll ḵ’áwa’wagaangaan.

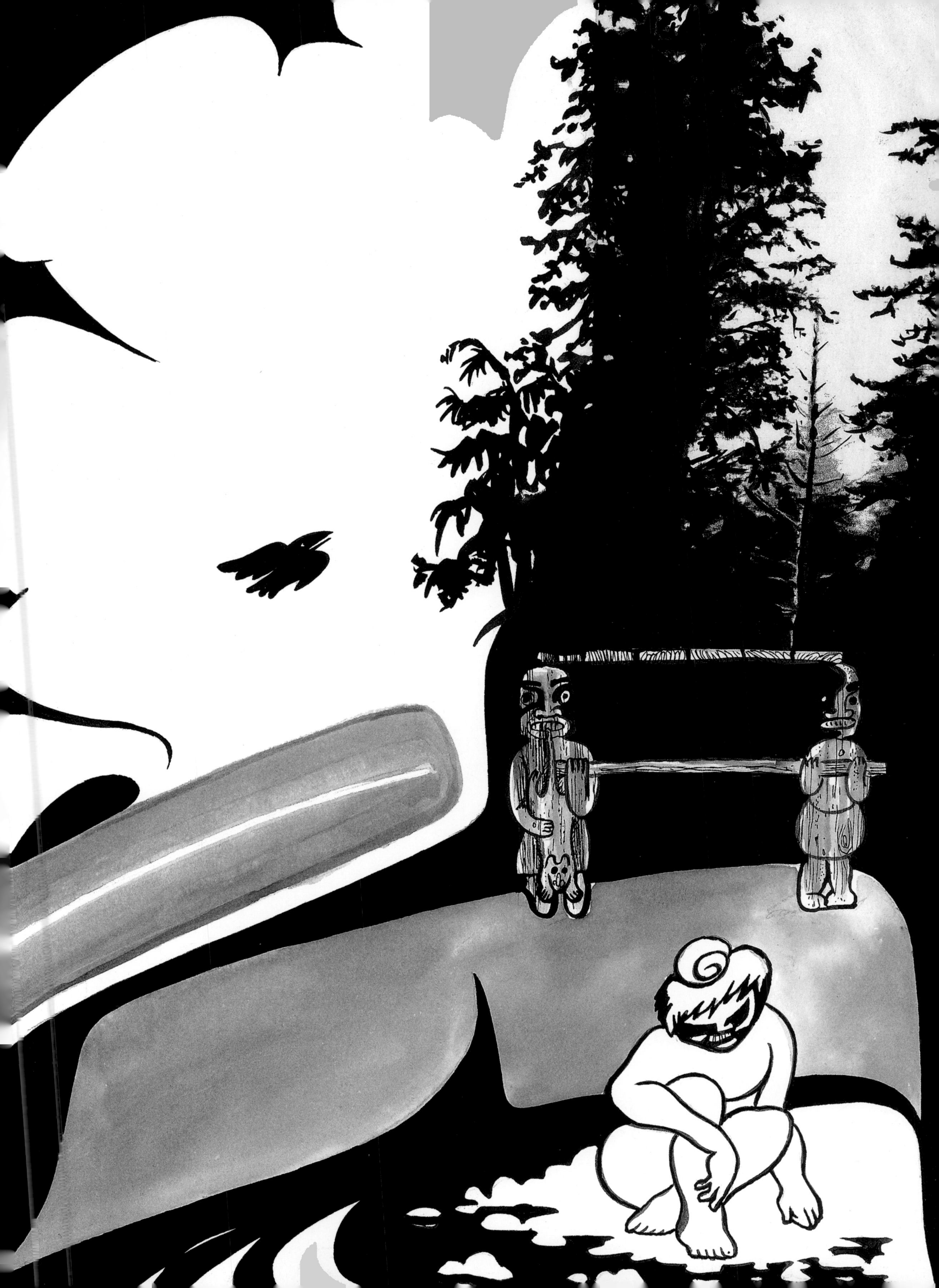

One evening, Elder heard a drum
sound, then saw a canoe carrying
four persons.
It came rapidly to the beach.

This canoe landed strangely
its bow striking the shore first.

OM: 'Waadluu sangnggyaa.yaan, gu 'la k̲'aw.a'wagandaan'aa.
'Waadluu ga ts'a.a sdansang 'la naas G̲aa giyaandaal.aan.

S: Gen singxii dii, hawx̲an ll k̲'aw.uu dii gan.
Gen tluu guuG̲a G̲a sdansing tluu k̲aatl'lx̲a xaang.ala,
gaguu 'la naa.uu dii gan.

K: 'Wáadluu sángyaayaan, gu 'll k̲'áwa'wagan dáan aa.
'Wáadluu ga ts'ée'ii sdánsang 'll náas G̲áa giyáandaalaan.

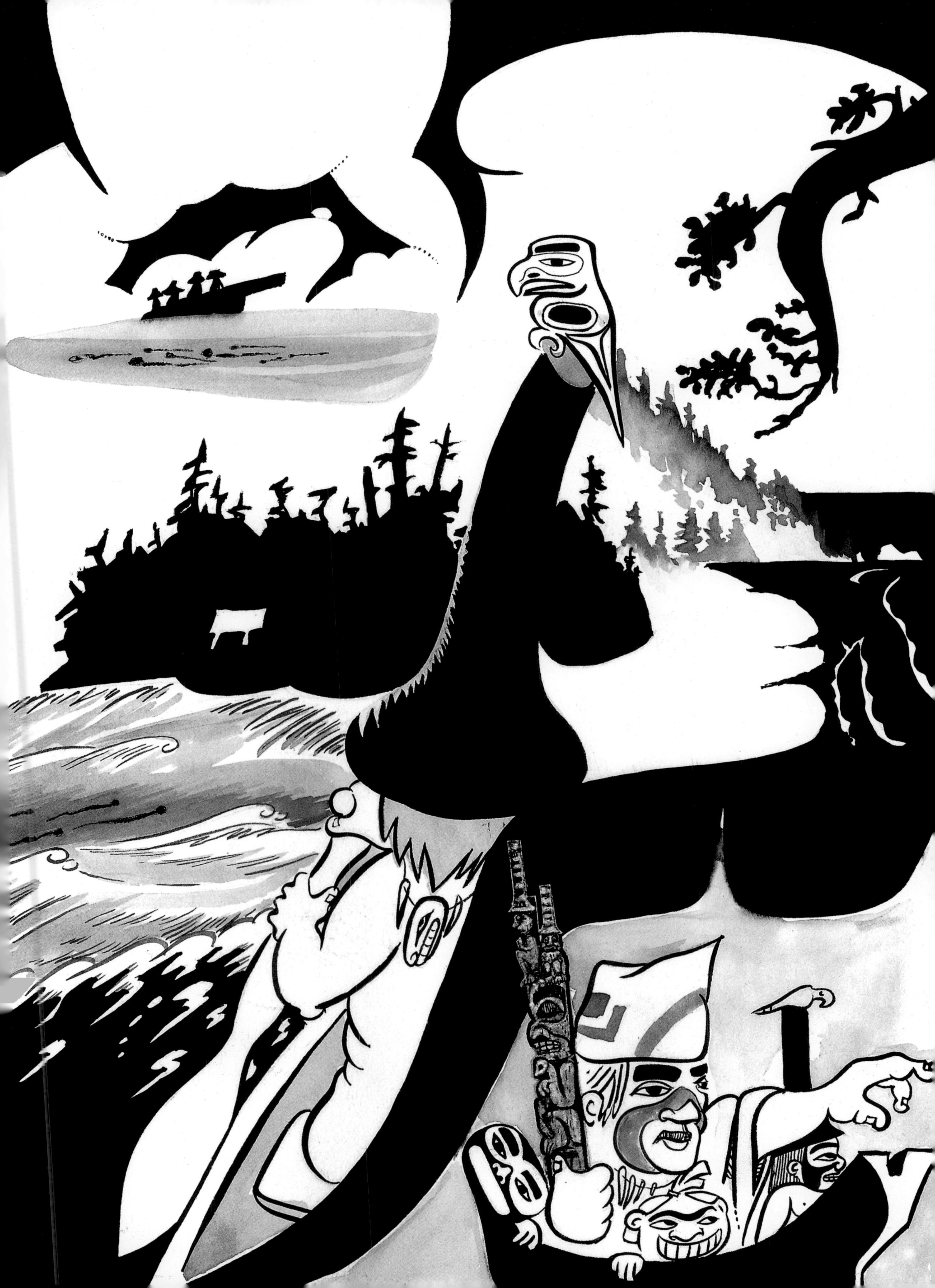

A shaman with a big hat sat in the middle of the canoe. He told the others, "Get off and go to the dead shaman."

Two paddlers ran into town.

OM: 'Waadluu yahgu 'laanaa dajang 'iiwaan ga̲a gut'ajaan.
Nang sg̲aagaa 'iiwaan.aan 'iijaan.
"Diid nang sg̲aagaa g̲ahlandaas x̲idgu hl g̲asgad.daa,"
hin 'la saawaan.
'Waadluu tlagu tl'a suus 'la gudang.gaanaan.
" 'Laa.aa hl k̲aahl," hin sk̲'ingnggwaa 'laanaa suudaayaan.

S: Nang x̲aayda yahguu daajing 'yuwan guut'as gan.
Nang sg̲aaga 'yuwan uu iijan.
"X̲idxuusda hla isg̲uu nang sg̲aaga iijin gina g̲aahlins
k̲ayd k̲'uuhlg̲a iijin," ll suu gan.
Gen g̲an ll unsiidan, tl'l suu gan.
"K̲aat'ahl hla, 'la g̲ahl hla is," kungii nang is g̲aa 'la suu.

K: 'Wáadluu yahgw 'láanaa dajáng í'waan g̲áa gut'ajaan.
Nang sg̲áagaa í'waanaan íijaan.
"Díid nang sg̲áagaa g̲ahlándaas x̲idgw hl g̲asgaddaa," hín 'll sáawaan.
'Waádluu tlagw tl'ä súus 'll gudánggaanaan.
" 'Láa aa hl k̲aahl," hín sk'íngnggwaa 'láanaa súudaayaan.

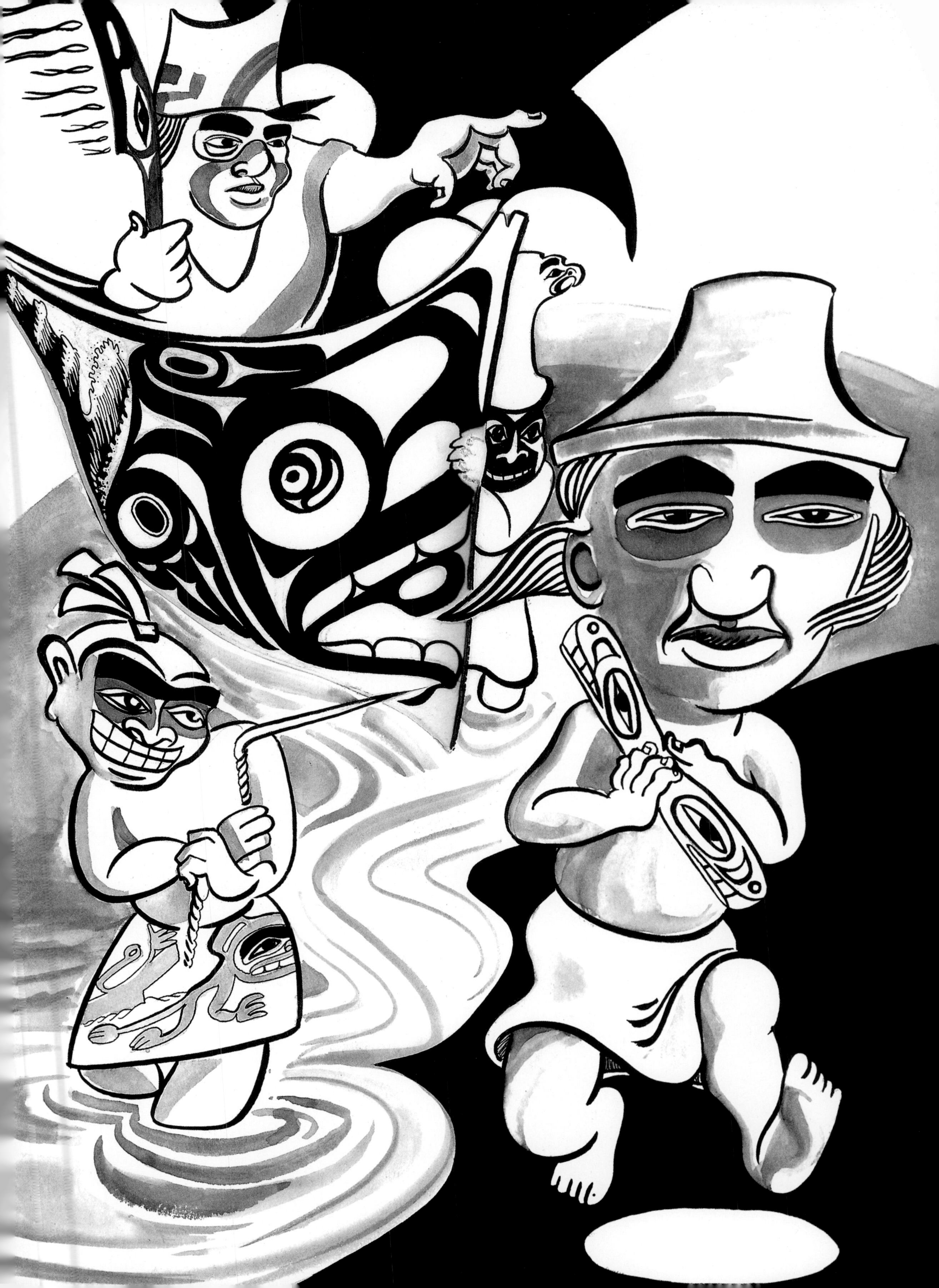

"The one we spoke through is not here."

"Go to the burial platform by the trees."

They didn't see Elder.
He saw them.
He understood them.

OM: 'Waa gingaan 'laa.aa 'la ḵak'aalaan. 'Laa x̲idgu 'la sdaaguhl Ḵ'awaas g̲am tl'a ḵingang.gaangaan.

S: Gen 'la G̲a 'la is gan. Ll hltaaxwii ll x̲idguu ḵ'aw.uu gan, g̲am 'la tl'l ḵing G̲ang gan.

K: 'Wáa gingáan 'łáa aa 'll ḵak'áalaan. 'Łáa x̲idgw 'll sdáaguhl k'áwaas g̲ám tl' kíng'anggaangaan.

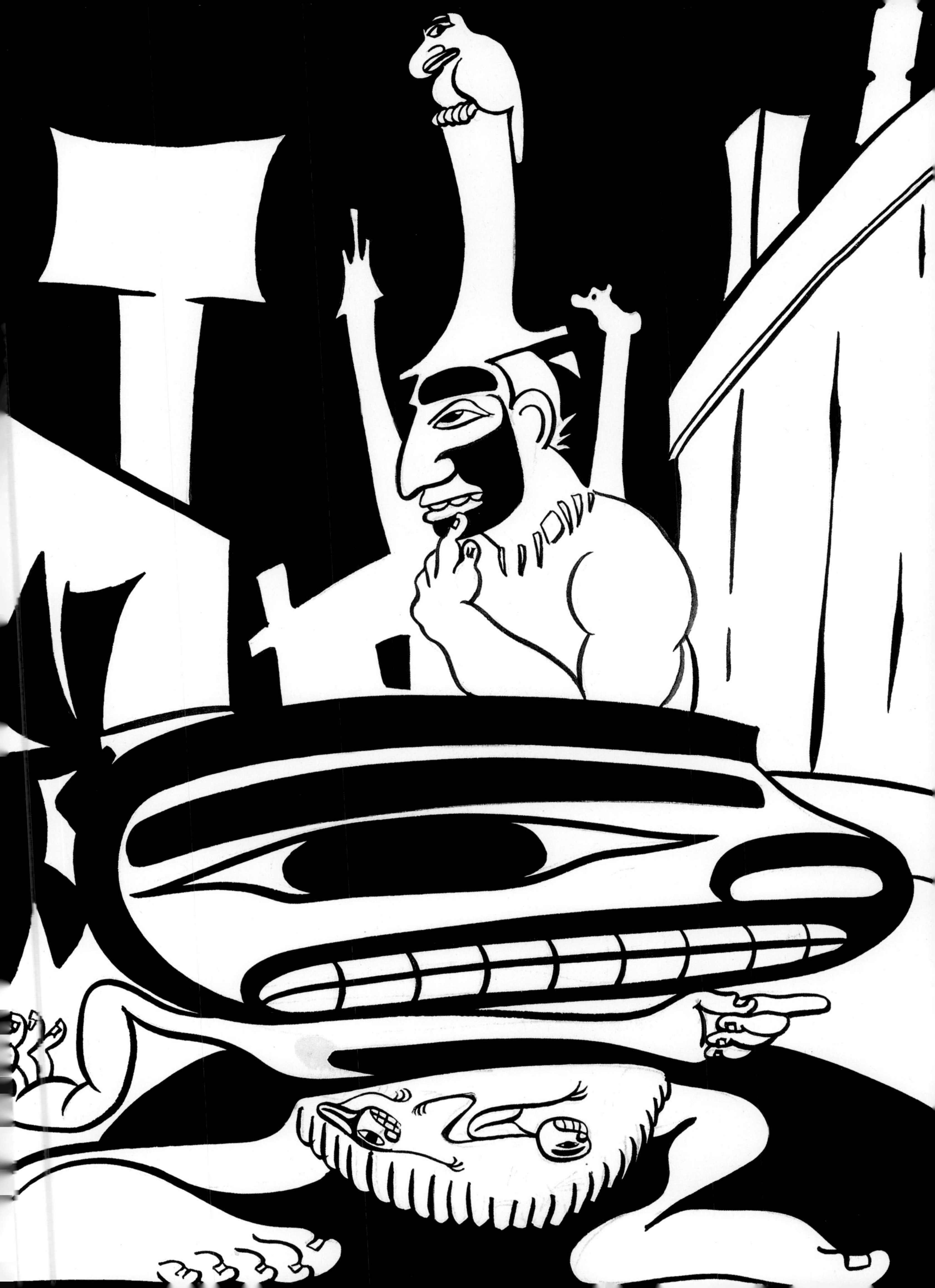

ᴏᴍ: ’Waadluu ’aa nang k̲a.aalaan ’aa nang k’ut’alaas k̲aj
’la dang k̲’ii.isalang.gaang.aan.
’Ahljii.uu ’la sdaaguhl ɢ̲aa k̲eewlaang.gaang.aan. ’Waagyaan ’la k̲’al
’Waasda ’laa ’la dang tl’ast’aayaan.

The two paddlers pulled the corpse
out of the coffin.
They wiggled the dead shaman’s head,
and pulled off the skin.

s: Gen ’waaniis k̲aat’ahl gan, nang k̲’uuda k̲aajii
’la da k̲’aayjuɢ̲alang gan.
Ll hltaaxwii uu k̲yahxuulang gan.
Gen ll k̲’al ’wasda ’la dantl’l gan.

ᴋ: ’Wáadluu aa nang k̲a’áalaan aa nang k’ut’áalaas k̲aj ’ll dáng
k̲’íi’isalanggaangaan.
Ahljíi uu ’ll sdáaguhl ɢ̲áa k̲éelaanggaangaan. ’Wáagyaan ’ll k̲’ál ’wáasdä
’láa ’ll dáng tl’ast’áayaan.

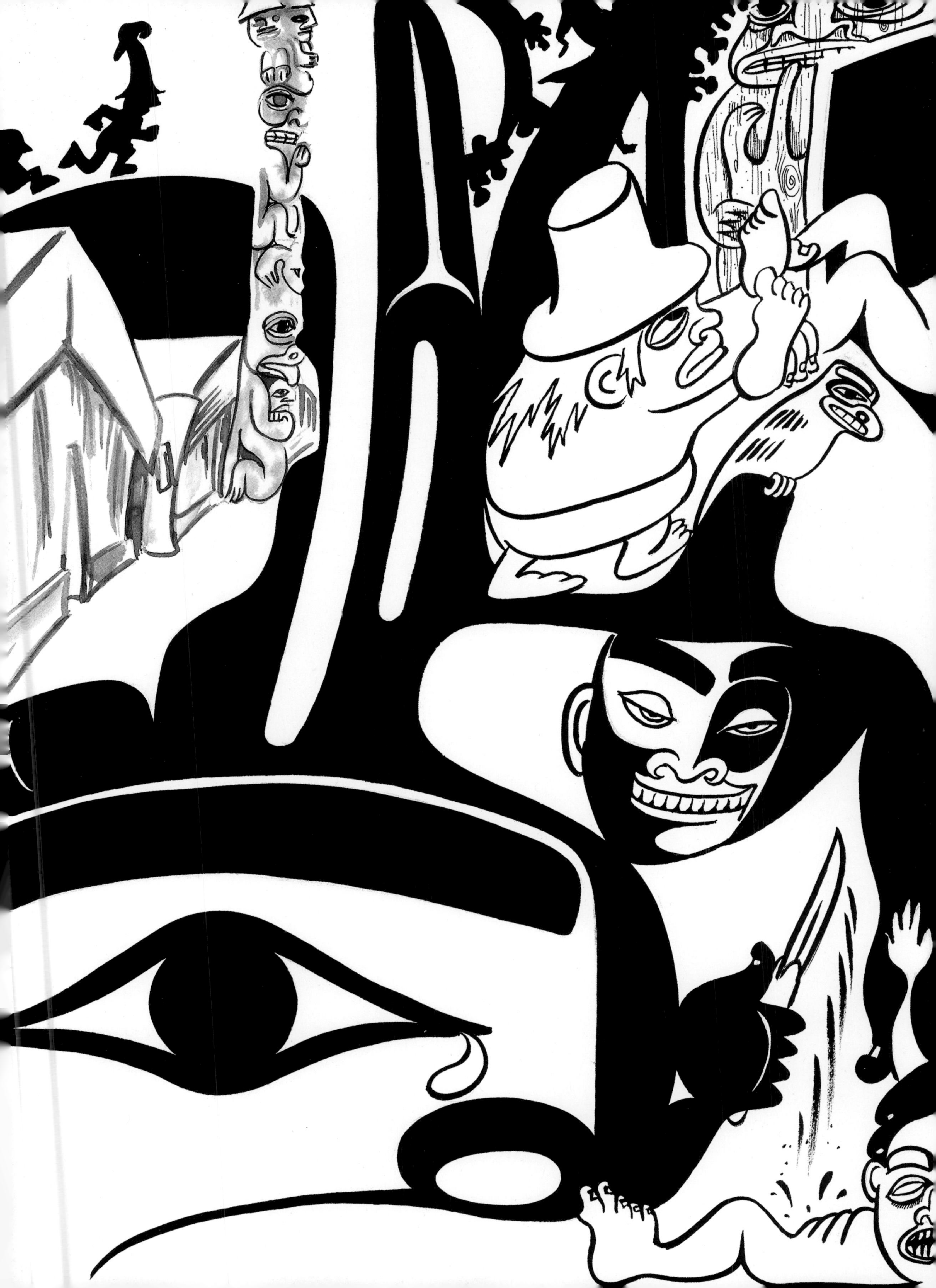

OM: ’Waadluu dang.ahl ’laa la k̲asaa.yaanii.
’Waagyaan ’la sdaaguhl hansan sdaaguhl.aang k̲’alga dlasgad.aan,
’laangaa tl’a tl’a.aadliisiidluu.
’Aa nang sɢ̲aagaa ’iiwaans tl’a sɢ̲aagaa k̲ald.uu ’la diing.gwaang.gaang.
aan, tl’a k’ut’ahlgiyaas gyaa’aa.
Tluugwee tl’aangaa ’la ’isda.gaang.aan k̲waan.aan.
’Waadluu ’aa nang sɢ̲aagaa ’iiwaans ts’ak’aa ’la ts’aandlii.gaan gam ’la
k̲aadliis ’laa tl’a k̲ing.’aang.aan.

They ran to the canoe with the skin.
Elder followed his friend.
Invisible.
They say.

The canoe started seaward,
with Elder in the stern.

S: Gen ɢandlaay ɢ̲a x̲iidgii ’la is gan.
Gen ll hltaaxwii ’laa.a k̲’al k̲ayts’id gan,
gen tllwaay guuɢ̲a k̲’al tl’l isda gan.
Nang sɢ̲aaga ’yuwan, sɢ̲aaga k̲’al gii ’la dáay.ying.gwang
gang giinii, nang sɢ̲aaga k̲’uuda gud.
Tllwaay ɢii k̲’al k̲waan ll isda gan.
Gen nang sɢ̲aaga ’yuwan ll sgwaagii k̲aadll gan,
gam ll k̲aadll tl’l k̲ing ɢ̲ang gan.

K: ’Wáadluu dángahl ’láa ’ll k̲asáayaanii.
’Wáagyaan ’ll sdáaguhl hánsan sdáaguhlaang k̲’álgä dlasgadáan,
’láangaa tl’ä tl’a’áadliisii dluu.
Aa nang sɢ̲áagaa í’waans tl’ sɢ̲áagaa k̲’áld uu ’ll diyínggwaanggaangaan,
tl’ä k’ut’ahlgiyáas gyaa aa.
Tlúu gwée’ee tl’áangaa ’ll isdägáangaan k̲wáanaan.
’Wáadluu aa nang sɢ̲áagaa í’waans ts’ak’ii ’ll ts’áandliigaan gám
’ll k̲áadliis ’láa tl’ä k̲íng’aangaan.

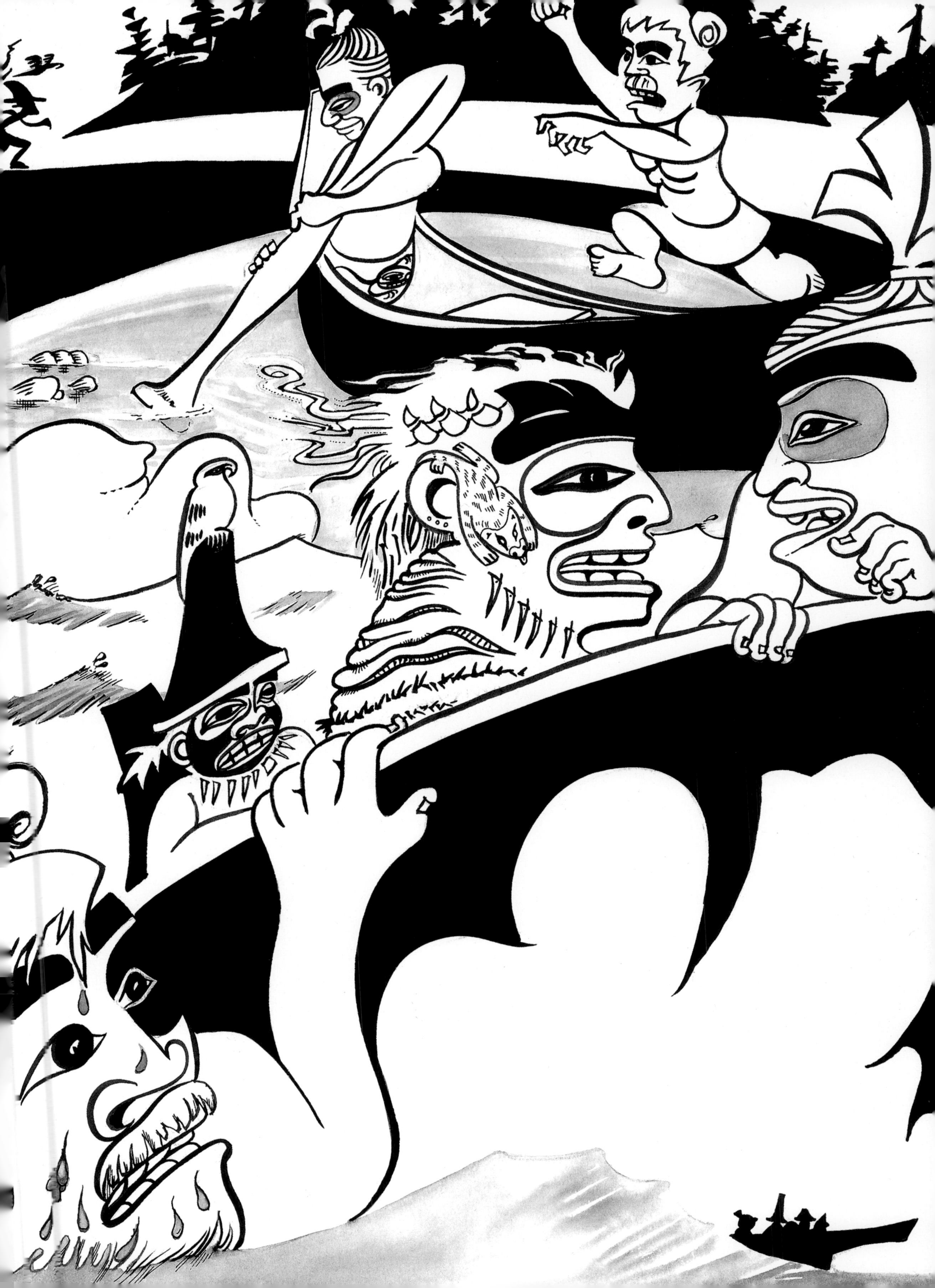

Elder saw that from the armpit of
each paddler,
hung something round.
He reached out,
touched one.
Grasped it.
Squeezed it.

OM: ’Waadluu k̲’ulang k̲ajang k̲un.aan ’laa ga ’la da xasgad.aan.

S: Gen k̲’uulang daanx̲an ’la gii ’la daa k̲’aasgid.

K: ’Wáadluu k̲’uláng k̲ajáng k̲unáan ’láagä ’ll da xasgadáan.

That paddler became ill.

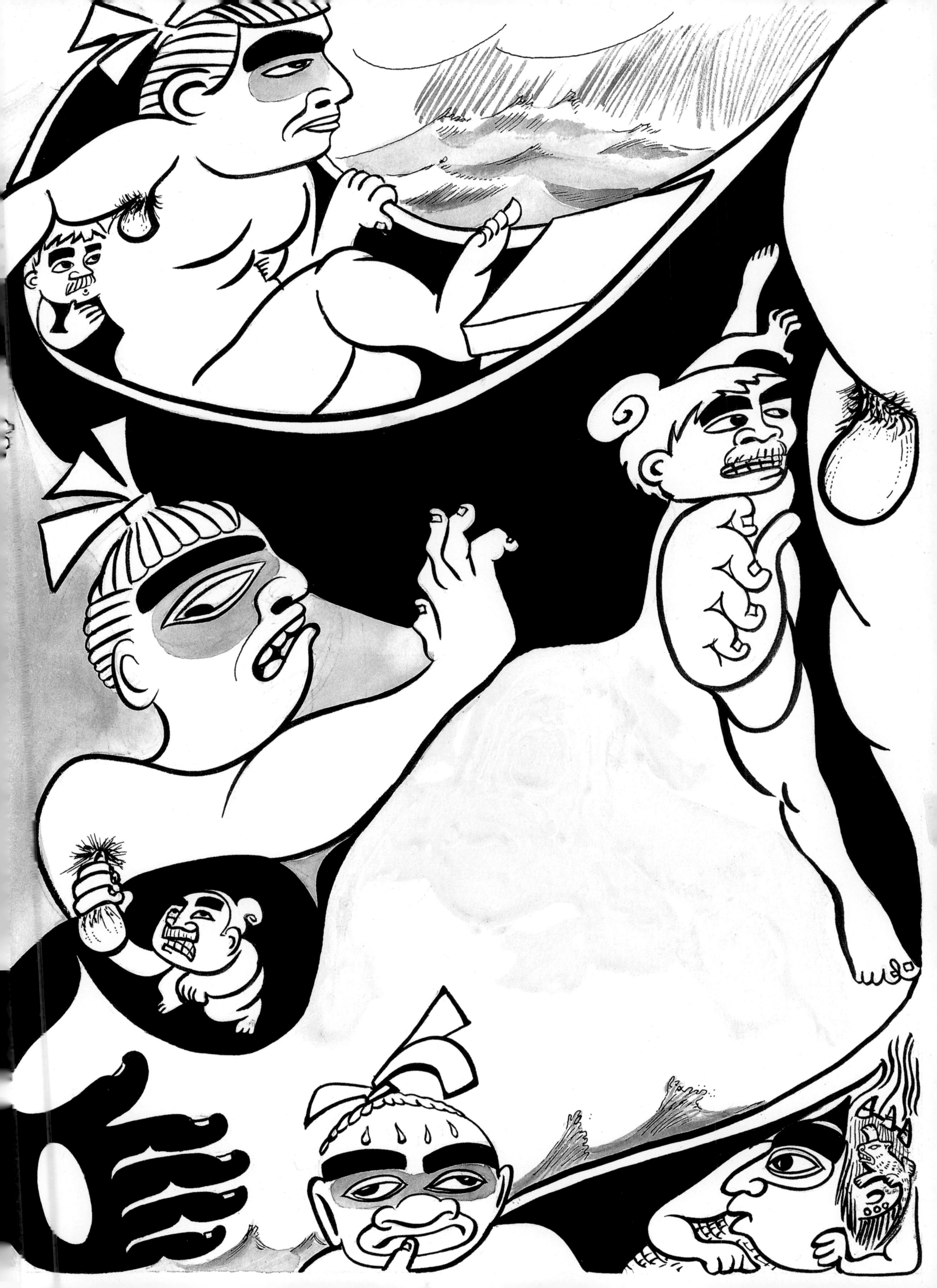

The Big Shaman
surrounded by many skins,
sat in the canoe.

Elder moved towards him.

OM: 'Waadluu 'la ḵ'uluu ḵaj xat'as.yaa 'laa gwa.agahl 'iiwaan.aan.

S: Gen ll sgwaay hldanxagang gan, gaguu ll ḵ'uuluu iijin guu.

K: 'Wáadluu 'll k'ulúu kaj xat'asyaa 'láa ɢwáagahl í'waanaan.

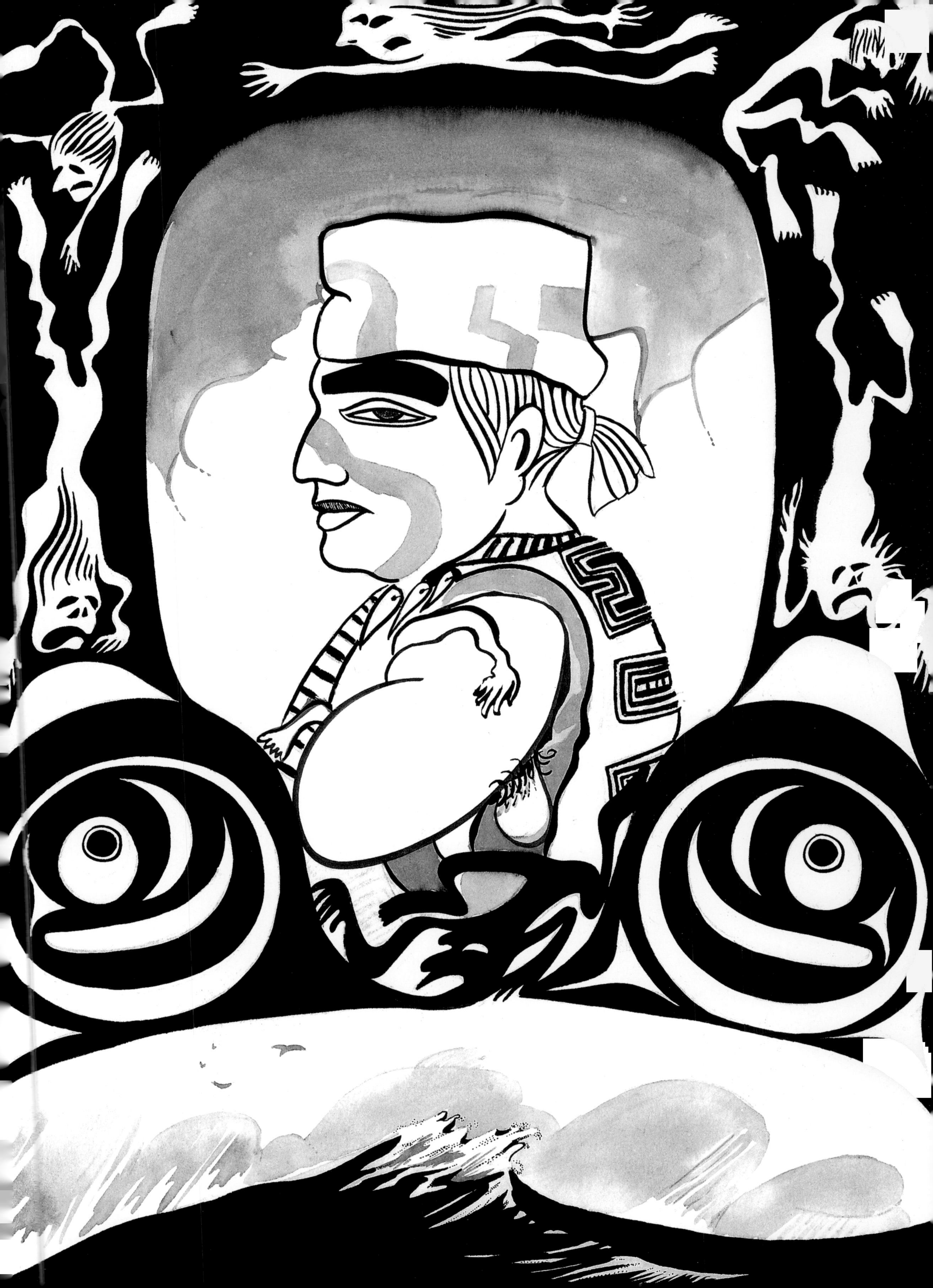

Elder grasped the Big Shaman,
squeezing the round thing in
his armpit.

The Big Shaman became ill.

OM: 'La gwa.agang.ḵawd hawisan 'laa sda 'aajgwii 'la G̱ut'agaan.aan.

S: G̱id ḵawdii ll hldanx̱agang, ising 'la sda 'laa G̱udts'ii gan.

K: 'Ll G̱wáagang ḵáwd háwsan 'láasdä áajgwii 'll gut'ägaanaan.

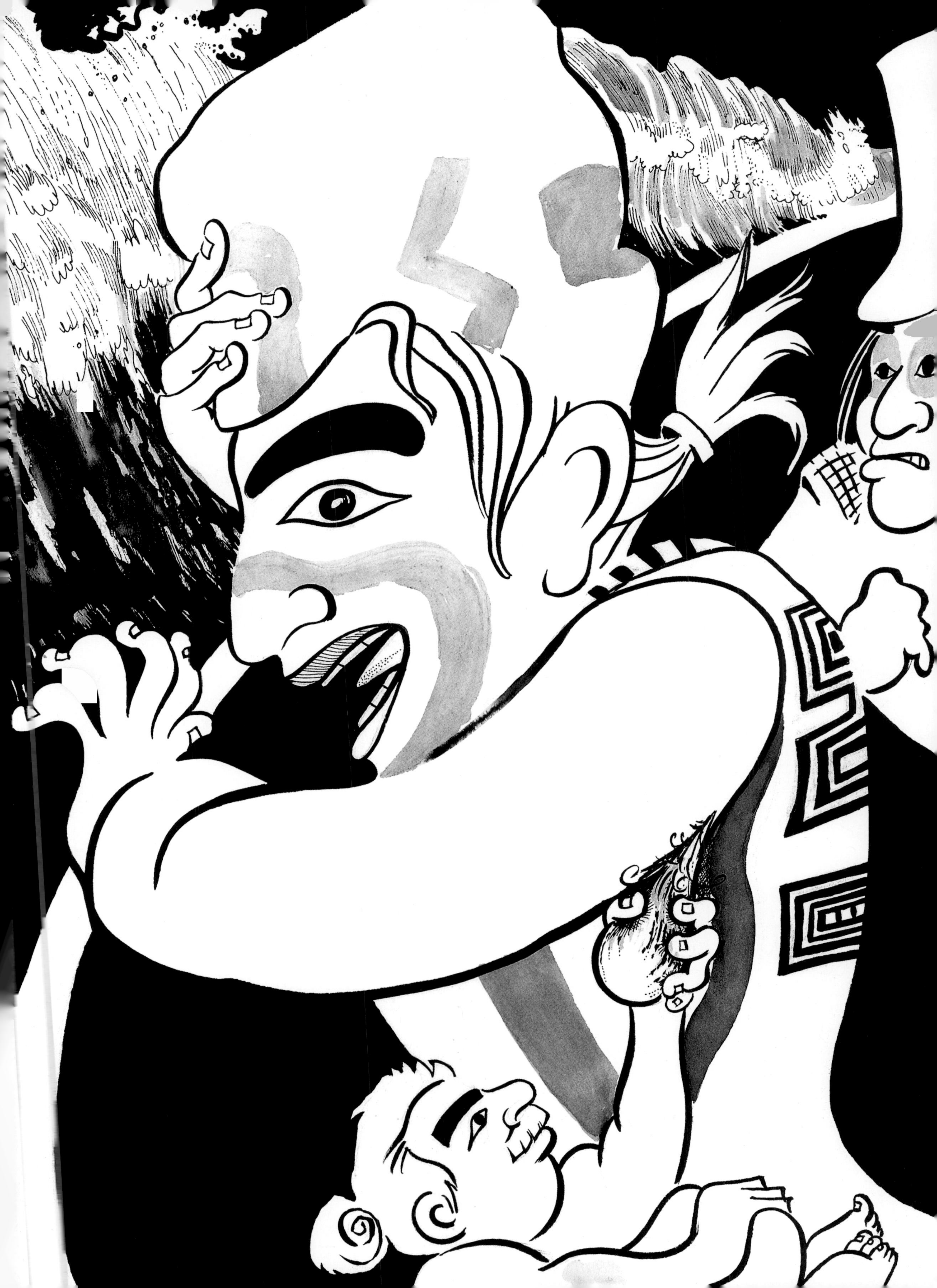

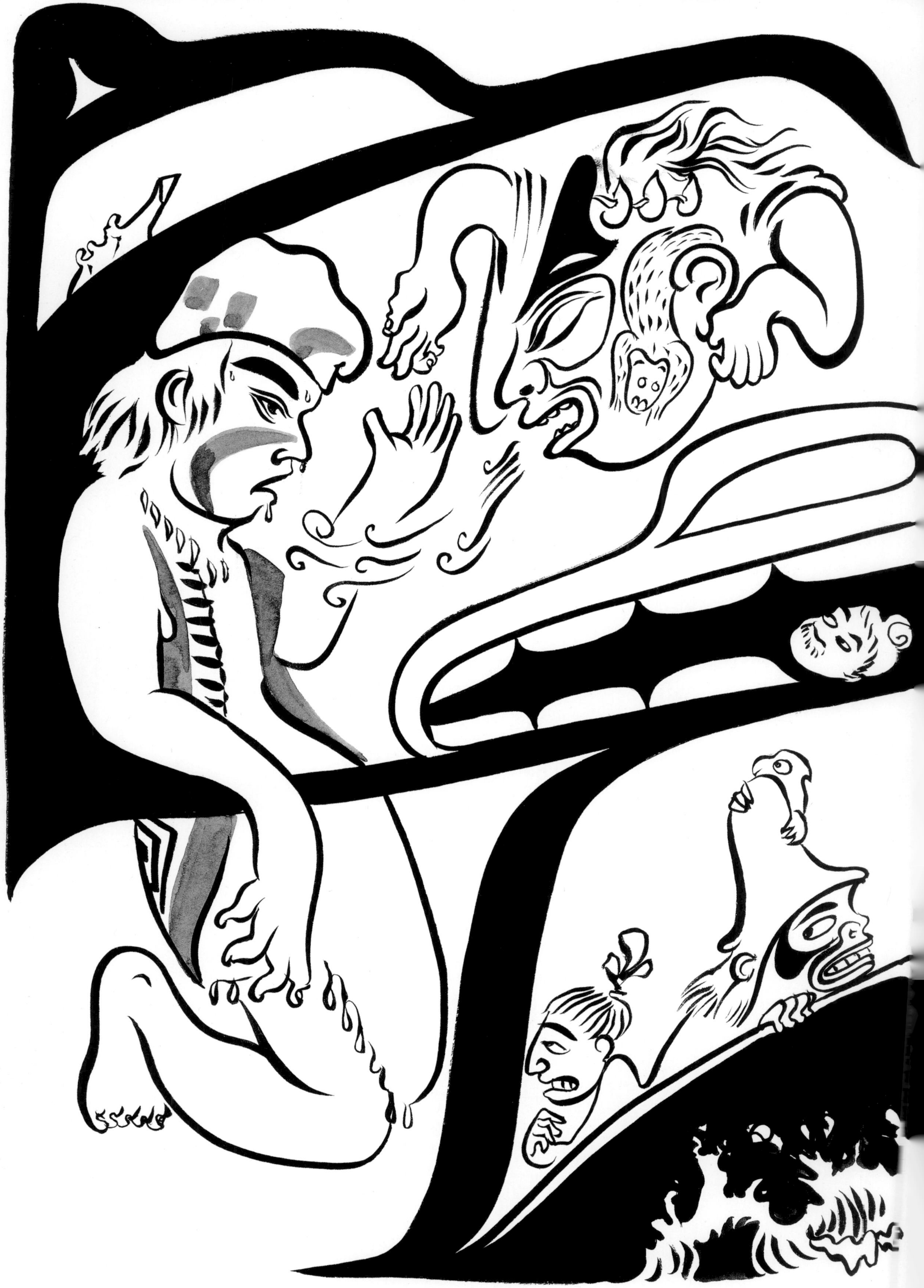

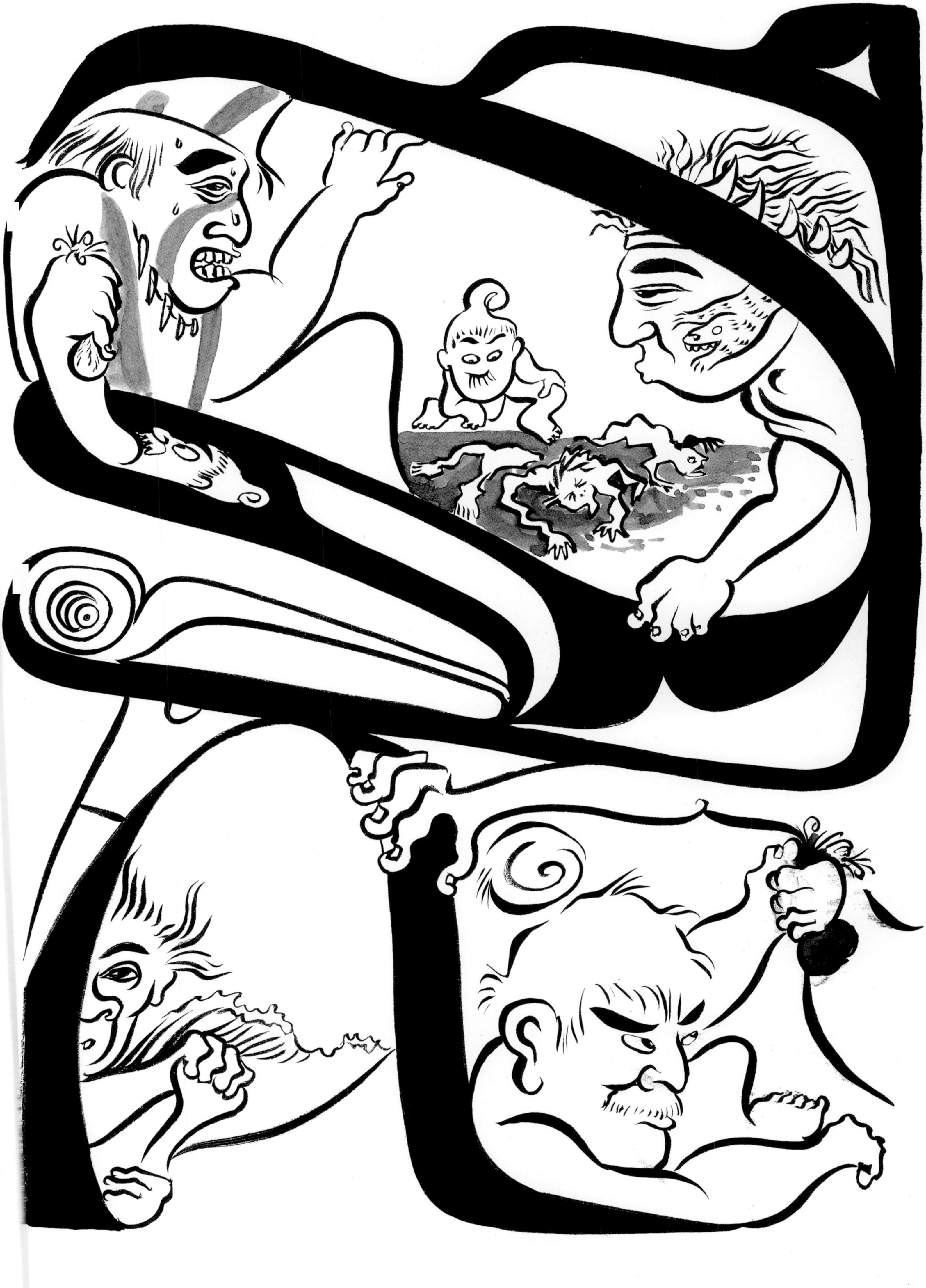

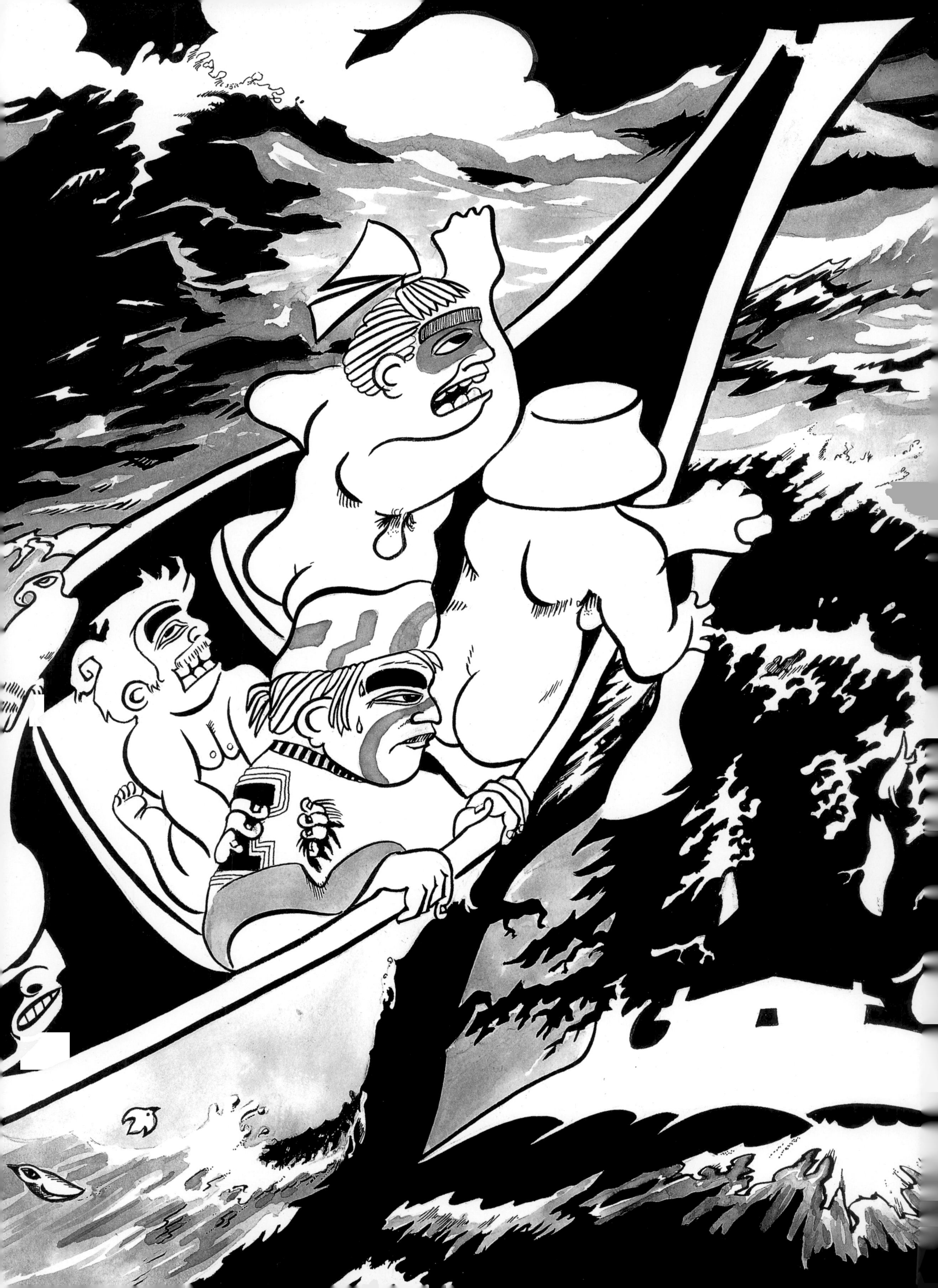

OM: "Hawiid hl dii dang ahl tluu ḵaa'wa," hin 'la suugaang.aan.

S: "Hawiid dii hla isda," ll suu gii.

K: "Hawíid hl díi dángahl tlúu ḵáa'uu," hín 'll súugaangaan.

All the paddlers tried to cure the
Big Shaman.
But as Elder continued to squeeze,
the Big Shaman began to die.

"Take me home."

The paddlers hurried.
Elder squeezed.

53

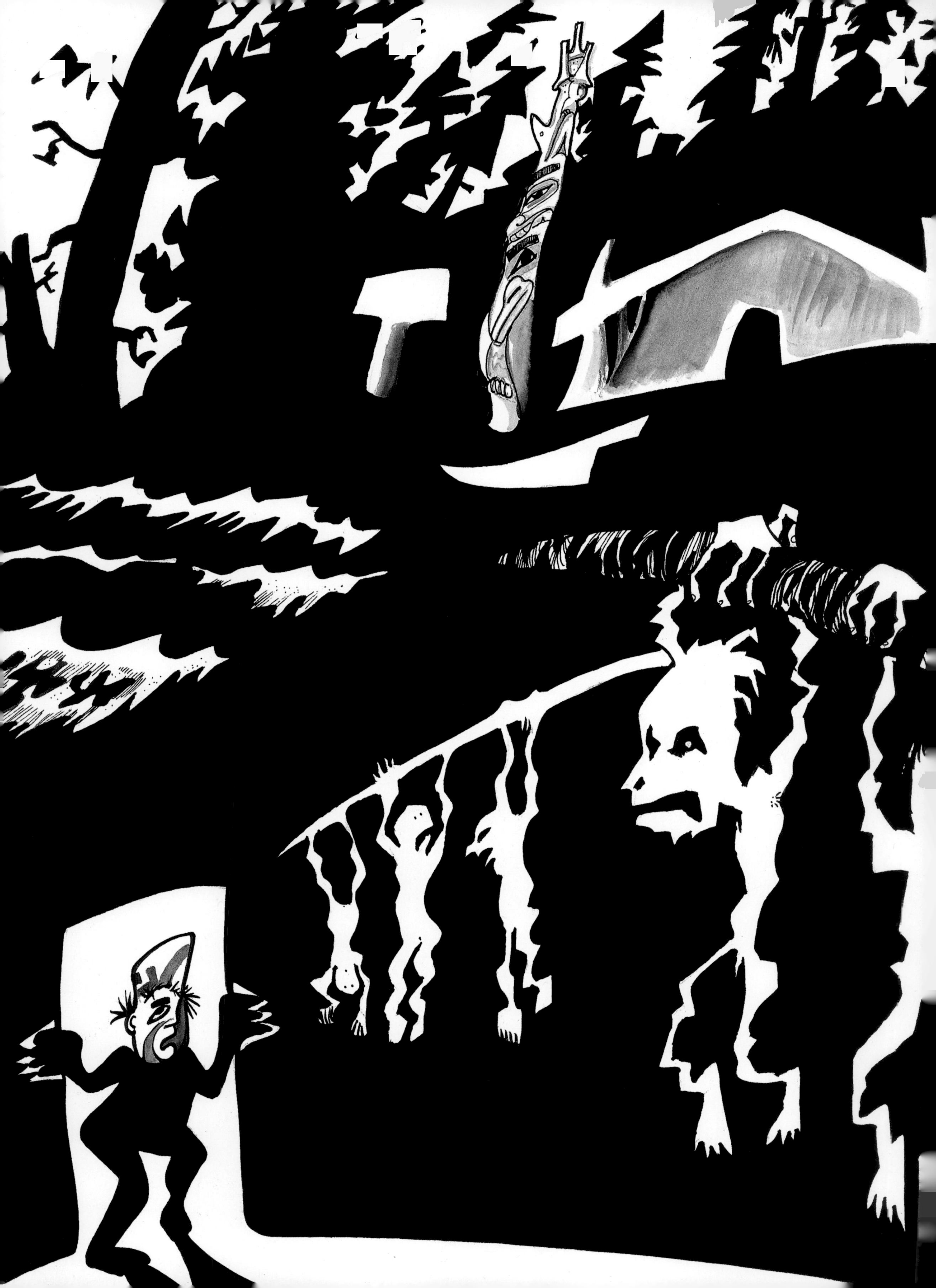

OM: ʼWaagyaan ʼlaa dangʼahl tlʼa G̲asgad.aan.
ʼWaagyaan tlʼa sG̲aagaa k̲ʼal tluu gwaa.a
k̲waans naaga tlʼa ʼisdaayaan.
ʼWaadluu ʼaa nang sG̲aagaa ʼiiwaans neeG̲ay ʼangaa k̲atsʼaayaan.

S: Gen ʼlaa.ad tlʼl isG̲uu gan.
ʼWagen sG̲aaga k̲ʼal k̲waans tllwaay
ʼwaasda naagaay G̲ii tlʼl isda gan.
Gen nang sG̲aaga ʼyuwan naagaay G̲ii ang.G̲a k̲aatsʼii gan.

K: ʼWáagyaan ʼláa dángahl tlʼä G̲asgadáan.
ʼWáagyaan tlʼä sG̲áagaa k̲ʼál tlúu gwaa
k̲wáans náagä tlʼä isdáayaan.
ʼWáadluu aa nang sG̲áagaa íʼwaans náay gii áangaa k̲atsʼáayaan.

They landed before the Shaman's house
and carried in the dead shaman's skin,
adding it the many others that
filled the house.

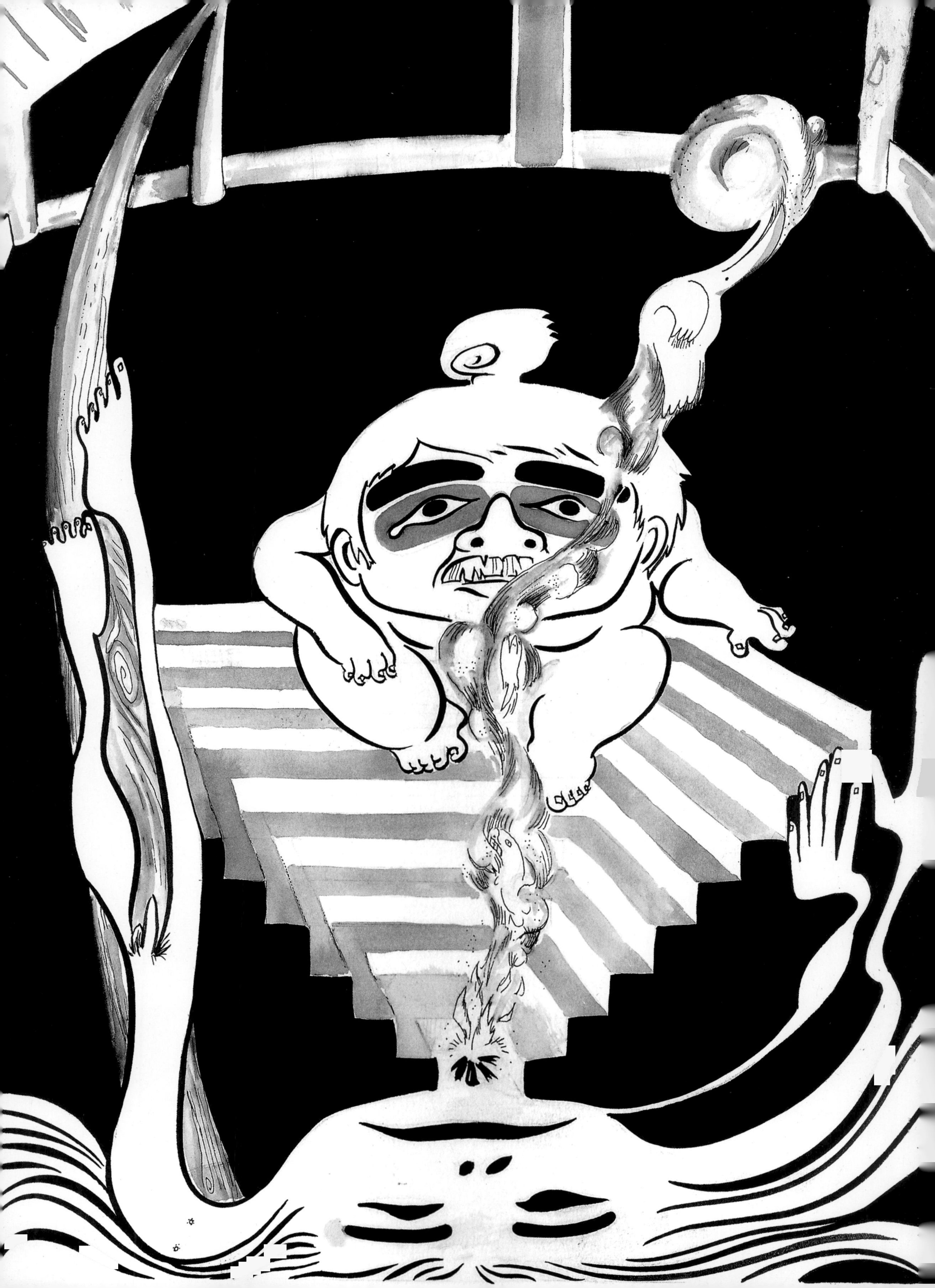

OM: 'Waagyaan 'la sdaaguhl k'al tl'a tl'aagahl sgyaan
Gahl 'la kak'aal.aanii.
Nee kaahlguud k'yuu ginn sk'agad sGwaanaang.aanii.
'Ahljii 'inguud 'waahl st'aawgaa.gaanii.
Kunasd han.uu 'aa.uu tlagu 'la'waagiigaang.aan.
"'Aajgwaa hl hawniis tl'iyuwada'waang,"
hin 'la sdaaguhl k'al tl'a suudaas 'la gudaang.aan.
'Waagingaan tl'aa'ilaa 'laa tl'a tl'ii'aaw.aan.

S: Naagaay Ga sahgii ll hltaaxwiis k'al tl'l isda,
'laa asing ad is gan.
Naay kaahlii gud k'yuu gina sGaagid sGwaanang gan.nii.
SGaaga k'al Ga st'aaxuuga gan.
Aaw tluu sGaaga 'yuwan gina isda jii.nga gan.
"Anis hla 'wahgwa giixii.aaw,"
ll hltaaxwiis k'al tl'l suu 'la guudang.
Gen 'la gyaaGa gudsda tl'l giixii.aaw gan.

K: 'Wáagyaan 'll sdáaguhl k'ál tl'ä tl'a'agahls gyáan
Gahl 'll kak'áalaanii.
Náay káahlguud k'yúu gin sk'agad sGwáanaangaanii.
Ahljíi íngguud 'wáa eehl st'aagáagaanii.
Kúnaasd hán uu aa uu tlagw 'll 'wáagiigaangaan.
"Áajgwaa hl hánas tl'iyuwadä'waang,"
hín 'll sdáaguhl k'ál tl'a súudaas 'll
gudáangaan.
'Wáa gingáan tl'aa iláa 'láa tl'ä tl'i'i'aawaan.

"Have that one hung over there."

Elder sat beside his friend's skin.

Again Elder attacked the Big Shaman.
Others were called to save him.
Still no one could see Elder.
They say.

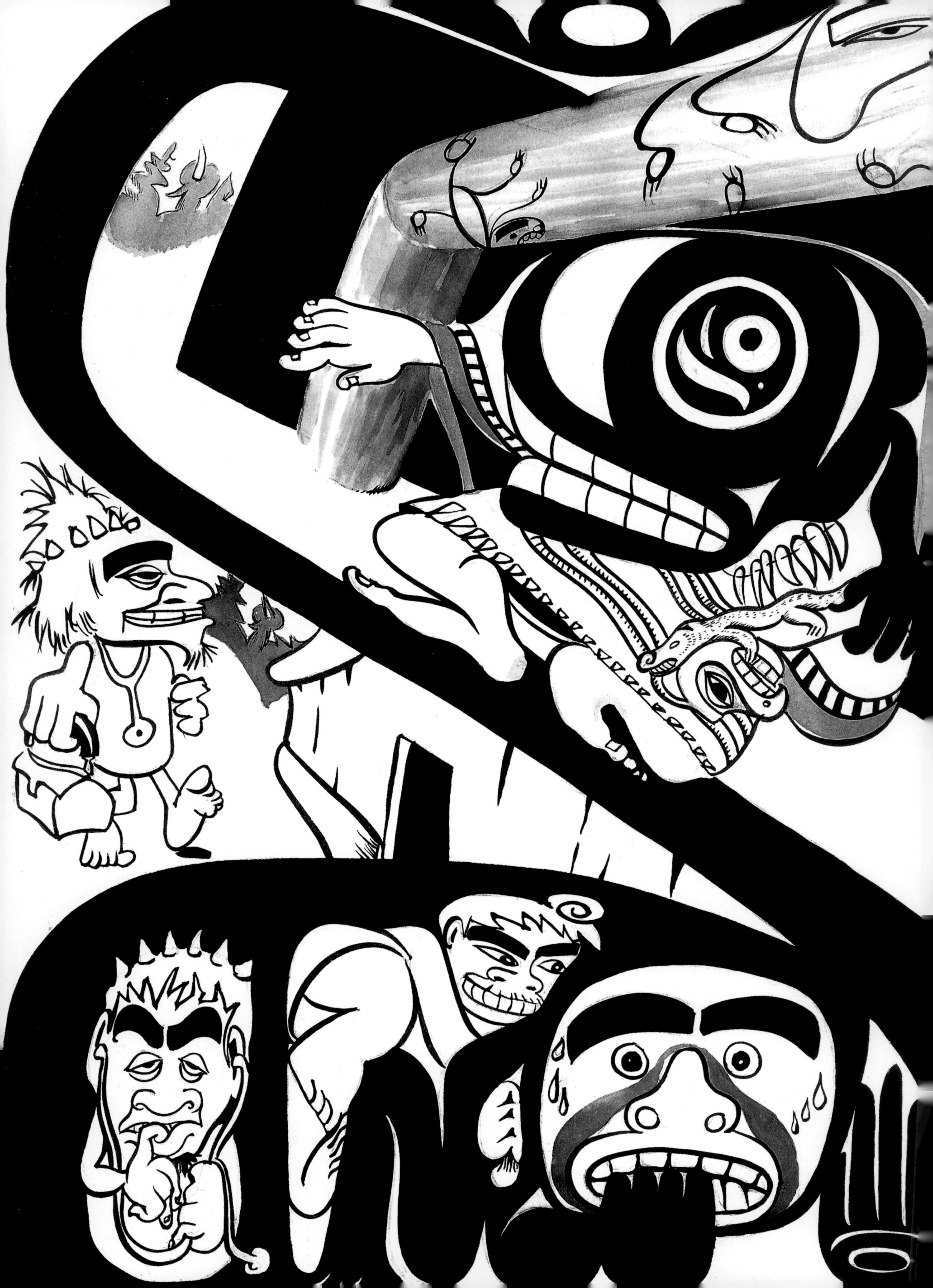

OM: 'Waadluu hawisan hit'an 'la k̲'aawaan.
'Waadluu hawisan 'la yahgusii 'laa 'la gijgiihldaas dluu k̲'ulang
kajang 'la sgwaay.ga 'la da xasgad 'iiwaangaang.aan.
'Waadluu 'la gwaagahl 'iiwaan.gaang.aan.
'Waadluu hit'an nang sG̲aagaa tl'a dliid 'yaan.aan.
'Waadluu 'laagaduu tl'a G̲id 'iiwaangaang.aan.
'Waagyaan 'la gwaagang.kawd sda gaang waanang 'laa 'la 'isdagaang.aan.
'Laa ts'ak'aa 'la k̲'aw.a'wagiiigaan.aan.
'La k̲agandaayeegaduu 'aa nang sG̲aagaas G̲isgaayaan.
'Waagyaan hawisan nang 'aadaa tl'a taanaa.aagaan.
'Ahl'aanii dangahl'isan 'laa k̲'hl tl'a G̲asgad.aan
'ahl 'aaniis hanisan 'laa G̲aduu G̲idgiigaang.aan.
'Waagyaan 'laa 'isan 'laa G̲aduu G̲isgaayaan.
Tl'a sG̲aagaa tlaa'ahl 'laa.an tl'a dla.aang.aan.
'Waak'yaahl ginggaang 'laa 'la dang dlagadgiigaangaan.
SG̲aagee tlaa'ahls dluu tl'a kayansdlaa.yaan.

S: Gen nang sG̲aaga 'yuwan ising k̲'aw.uu gan.
Gen ising ang.G̲a yahguusii 'la giijiigihlda gan,
ang.G̲a k̲'uulang ll sgwaay guu 'la daasgid 'yuwan
'waadahlG̲a gaa.ngang.
Gen 'waadahlG̲a gaa.ngang ll sgwaay hldanx̲agang gan.
Gen nang sG̲aaga tl'l sG̲aw gen 'la tl'l daw gan.
'La gud 'la tlaaG̲anang G̲udsdll gan.
Ll hldanx̲agang sda 'wahgwii agang sda 'la 'la daats'ii gan.
Jii.nga ll sgwaay guu 'la k̲'aw.uu gan.
Aniis sG̲aaga gam ll k̲aaganda G̲ang gan.
Ising nang aadaga asing 'laa gii tl'l sG̲aw guuda gan.
Ll daanaay guu tl'l isG̲uu gan, 'waaniis ad uu.
'Waaniis asing 'la G̲aaduu hlG̲ang.gulx̲a jii.nga gan.
'Laa asing G̲a jiiG̲aayG̲a gan.
SG̲aaga tlaa.ahl asing 'la G̲an tl'l sG̲aw gan.

K: 'Wáadluu háwsan hat'án 'll k̲'áawaan.
'Wáadluu háwsan 'll yahgwsíi 'láa 'll gijgíihldaas dluu k̲'uláng
kajáng 'll sgwáaygä 'll da xasgad í'waangaangaan.
'Wáadluu 'll G̲wáagahl í'waangaangaan.
'Wáadluu hat'án nang sG̲áagaa tl'ä dli'idyáanaan.
'Wáadluu 'láa G̲adúu tl'ä G̲id í'waangaangaan.
'Wáagyaan 'll G̲wáagang káwdsdä gáang wáanang 'láa 'll isdägaangaan.
'Láa ts'ak̲'íi 'll k̲'áawägiiigaanaan.
'Ll kagándaayee G̲adúu aa nang sG̲áagaas G̲isgáayaan.
'Wáagyaan háwsan nang k̲'álaad tl'ä táanaa'aagaan.
Ahl'áanaa dángahl isan 'láa k̲'uhl tl'ä G̲asgadáan
Ahl 'áanaa hánïsan 'láa G̲adúu G̲idgïigaangaan.
'Wáagyaan 'láa ïsan 'láa G̲adúu G̲isgáayaan.
Tl'ä sG̲áagaa tláahl 'láa an tl'ä dla'áangaan.

The people called one shaman to help.
Then they called nine others.
Still, no one was able to save the
Big Shaman.

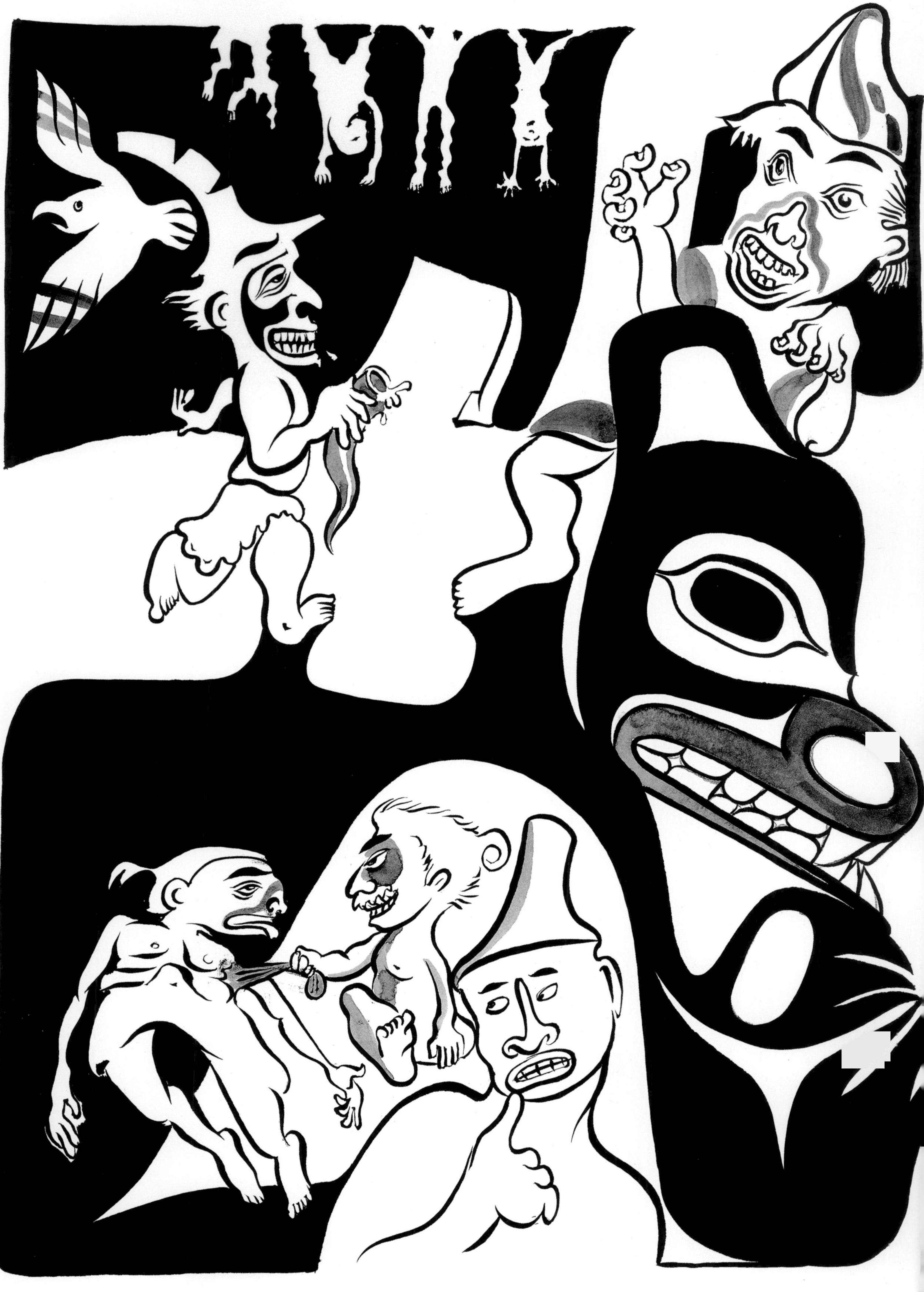

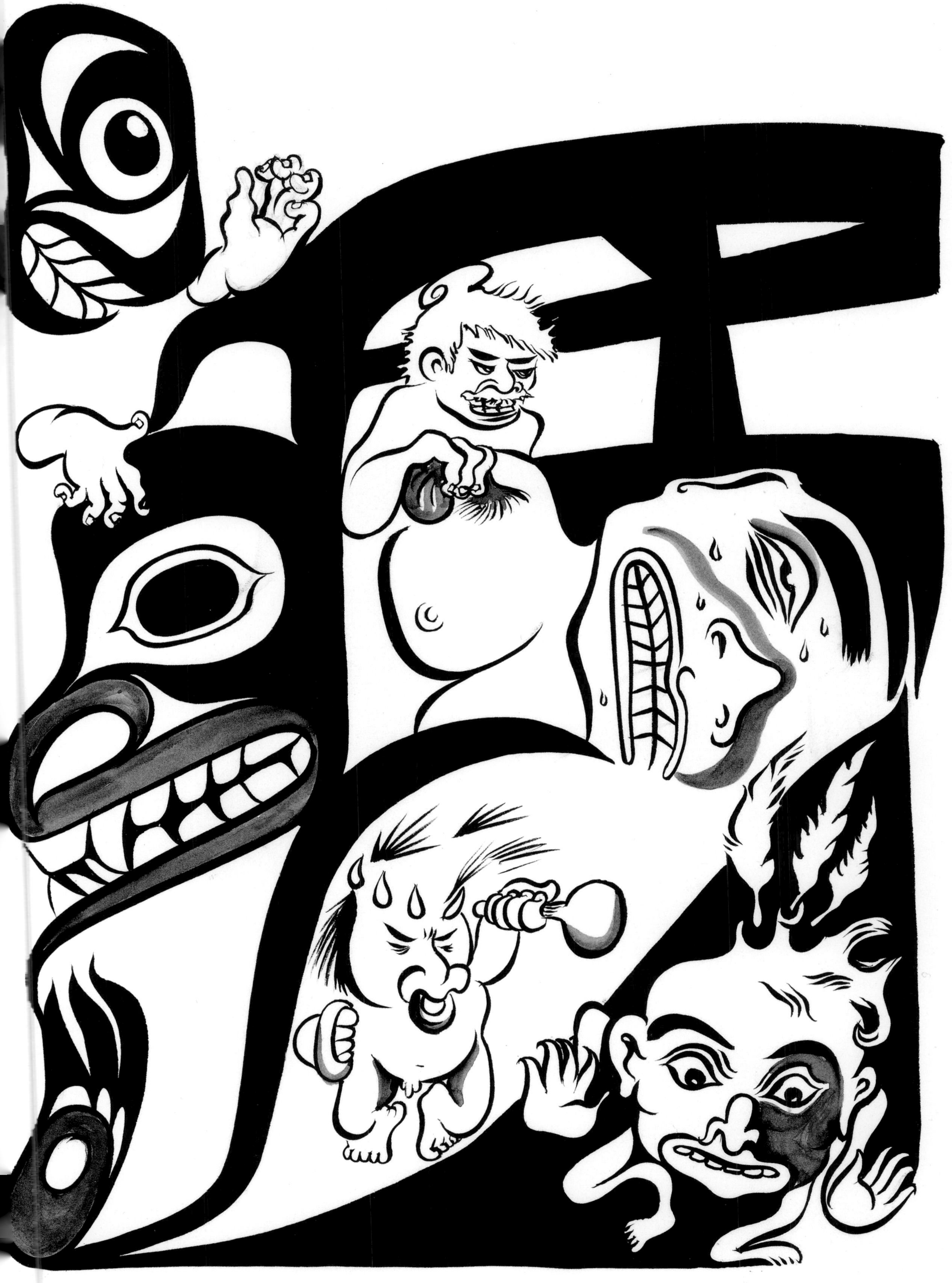

OM: ’Waak’yaahl ginggaang ’laa ’la dang dlagadgiigaangaan.
SGaagee tlaa’ahls dluu tl’a kayansdlaa.yaan.
SGaan ga sangaagins tl’a taan.aa.aagaan.
’Waadluu ’laa dang ahl tl’a Gasgad.aan.
Hawaan waajgwaa Gagwii ’la tluu kaagandaan ’aa nang sGaagaas ts’ak’aa ’’aa nang sGaagas k’awaas ’la keengaan.
’La sdaaguhl k’al ’la dla.aadliis Gahl.uu st’ii sang’iits’aa ’laa ga ’la ’isdaayaan.

Then they called for Spirit Dangerous to Offend.

From her canoe, she could see Elder sitting behind the Big Shaman.

S: Jii.nga ging.gang ’la ’la dang dllt’as gan.
Gen ga sGaaga tlaa.ahl Gihl gen, tl’l kaayinsdll gan.
SGaagaGwa Sangaagins tl’l taanGa gan.
’Waadluu ’la dang.ad tl’l isGuu gan.
’Waadsxwa Gaagwii hawxan tluu guuGa ’la tluu kaaging dluu, nang sGaaga ’yuwan sgwaagii nang sGaaga k’aw.uu ’la king gan.
Ll hltaaxwiis k’al ’la isda gan, Gaagan ’la gii daanxan st’ii tlaats’iiga ’la isda gan.

K: ’Wáak’yaahlg ginggáang ’láa ’ll dáng dlagadgíigaangaan.
SGáagaay tláahls dluu tl’ä kayánsdlaayaan.
SGáan ga sangáagans tl’ä táanaa’aagaan.
’Wáadluu ’láa dángahl tl’ä Gasgadáan.
Hawáan wáajgwaa Gagwíi ’ll tlúu káagan dáan, aa nang sGáagaas ts’ak’íi aa nang
SGáagaas k’áwaas ’ll kéengaan.
’Ll sdáaguhl k’ál ’ll dla’áadliis Gahl uu st’íi sang’íits’aa ’láagä ’ll ’isdáayaan.

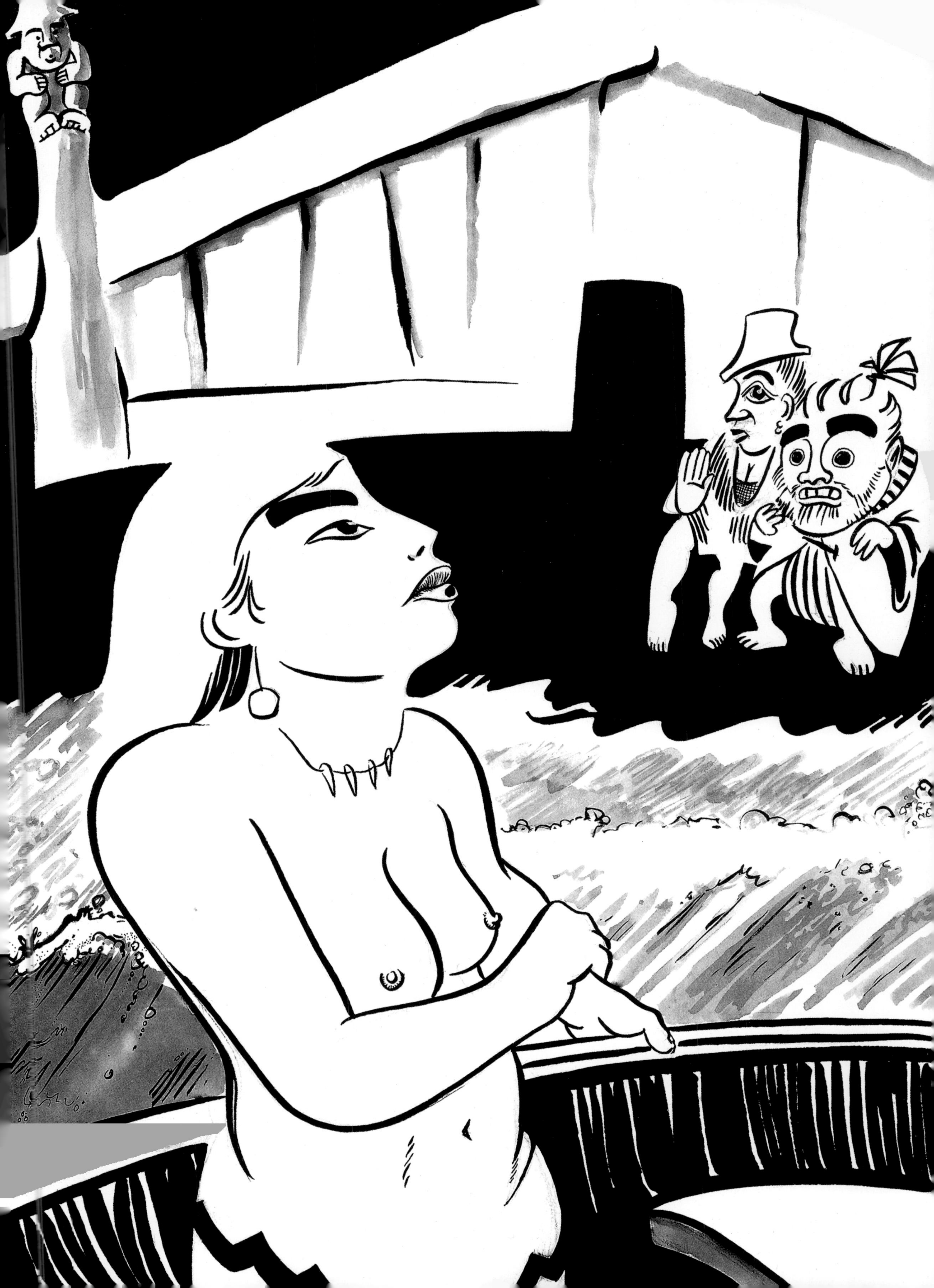

She came to the door,
and spoke directly to him.

"Don't embarrass me and I will
speak through you."

OM: ʼWaadluu ʼaa nanag sG̲aagaas G̲asgadsdluu naaga ʼla k̲atsʼaayaan.
ʼWaadluu ʼlaa tsʼakʼaa ʼla k̲ʼawaas ʼlaa ʼla k̲eengaan.
"Hl k̲atsʼaasdluu dii x̲ang G̲as hl k̲aa.ang,"
hin ʼlaa ʼla suudaayaan.
"ʼWaagyaan dan.ii hl suu.asgaa," hin ʼla saawaan.

S: Aniis sG̲aaga isG̲uu gan dluu, naahgii ʼla k̲aatsʼii gan.
Gen ll sgwaagii ʼla k̲ʼaw.uu ʼla k̲ing gan.
"Hll k̲aatsʼii gen, gam dii G̲iidax̲asdll daG̲ang,"
ʼla ʼla suuda gan.
Gen dang gud hll kihlgulas ga," ll suu gan.

K: ʼWáadluu áa nang sG̲áagaas G̲asgads dluu náagä ʼll k̲atsʼáayaan.
ʼWáadluu ʼláa tsʼakʼii ʼll k̲ʼáwaas ʼláa ʼll k̲éengaan.
"Hl k̲atsʼáas dluu díi x̲áng G̲as hl k̲áaʼang," hín ʼláa ʼll súudaayaan.
"ʼWáagyaan dáng íi Hl súusaang," hín ʼll sáawaan.

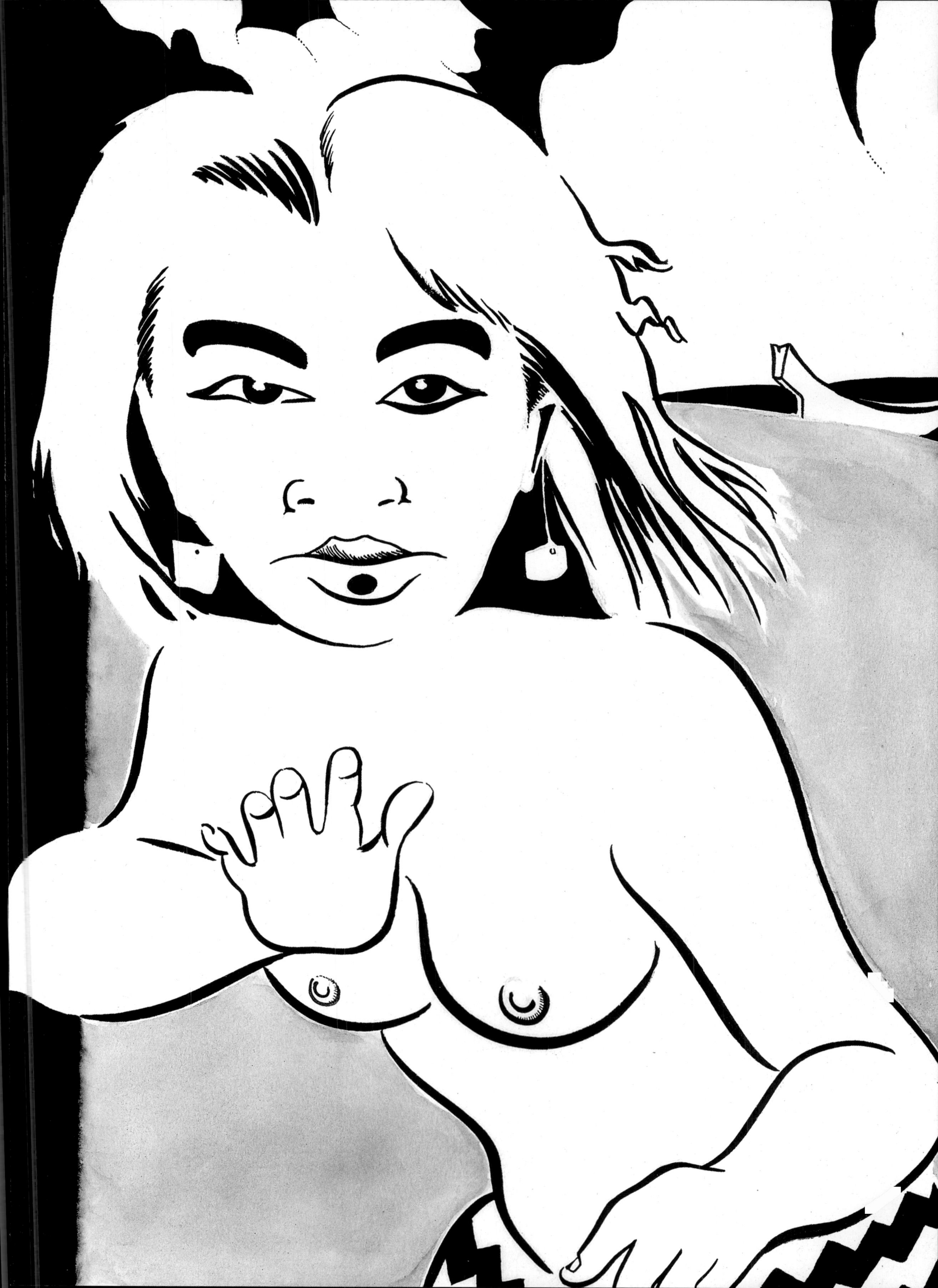

Spirit Dangerous to Offend began
to perform.
Elder let go of the Big Shaman.
The people said to give the unseen
spirit what he wanted.
And so they gave him a box of property.
They gave him his friend's skin.

Spirit Dangerous to Offend put Elder
and the skin into a woven mat
and carried him outside.

OM: 'Ahljii ahl.uu tlaan 'laa 'la G̲iyhldaayaan. 'Waagyaan 'la k̲agaanaan.

S: G̲aagan.uu 'la sG̲un 'la t'aasdll gan. Gen ll k̲aagan gan.

K: Ahljíi eehl uu tláan 'láa 'll G̲íiyhldaayaan. 'Wáagyaan 'll kag̲áanaan.

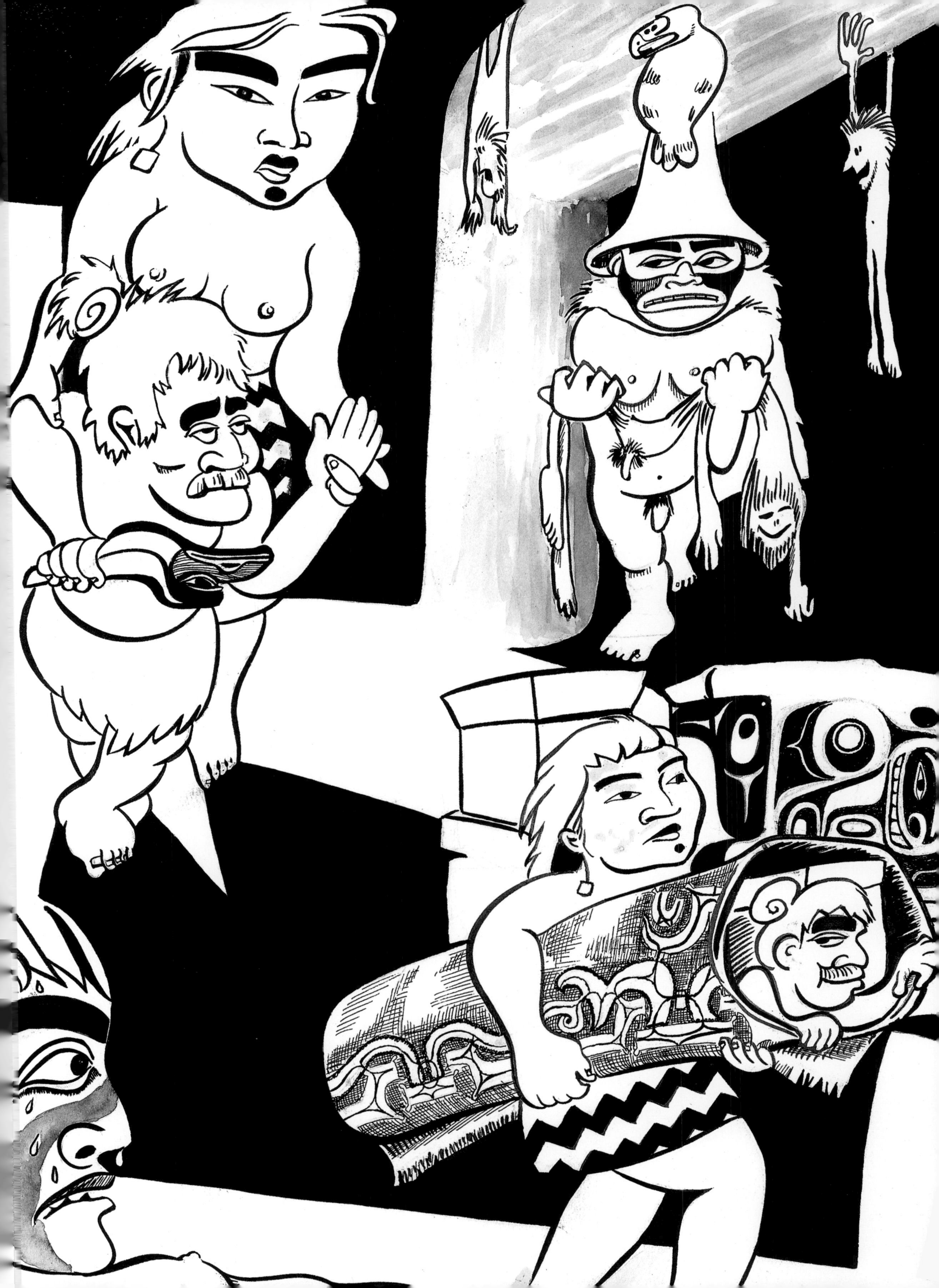

Once outside, she told Elder,

"I will cause a sickness,
and if they do not call you,
let them die."

"If they call you, and they pay you,
you may cure them."

OM: 'Waagingaan 'lee.ee 'la suuidaan.
'Waagyaan sGaan ga sangaagins sahlgaan tluu ḵaaydaan.
X̱aadgee ḵwaanaanii.

S: Gen, 'la gud 'la kihlgul xidii.
'Wagen SGaanaGwa Sangaagins sdiihl gan.
Gud ad ḵiiGawa ḵwaan 'la daaGa gan.

K: 'Wáa gingáan 'lée'ii 'll súuïdaan.
'Wáagyaan sGáan ga sangáagans sahlgáang tlúu ḵáaydaan.
X̱aadgáay ḵwáanaan ii.

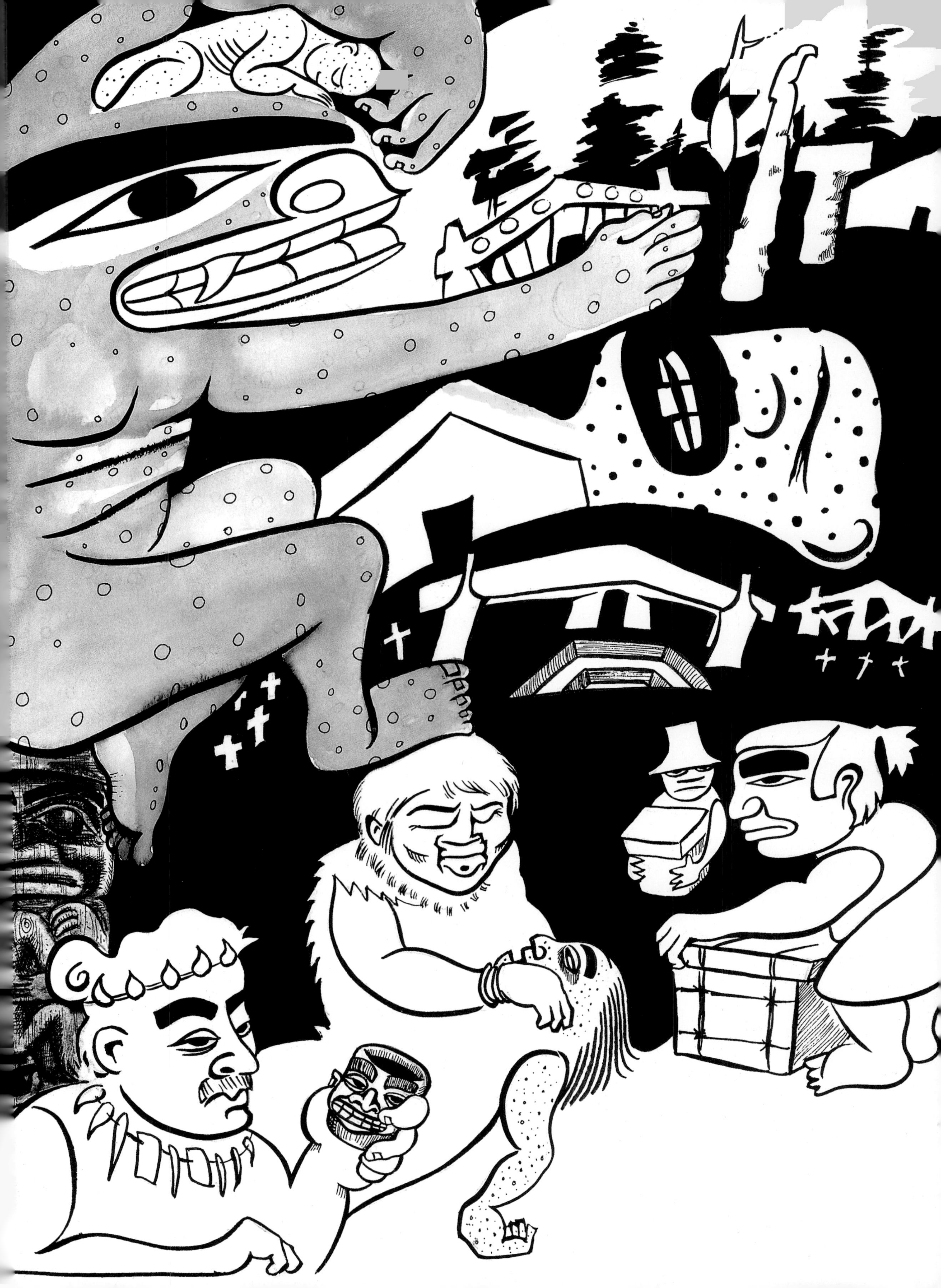

Elder understood.

**Spirit Dangerous to Offend carried
him back to Sk'a.aaws.**

OM: 'Waadluu hit'an 'aa nang sɢaagaas ɢiiy 'la suu saangaan gingaan
'lee.ee 'la saawaan.

S: Gen 'la king.ɢuu 'la nang sɢaaga gud 'la suu gan,
'la gud 'la kihlgul gan.

K: 'Wáadluu hat'án áa nang sɢáagaas ɢíi 'll súusaangaan gingáan
'lée'ii 'll sáawaan.

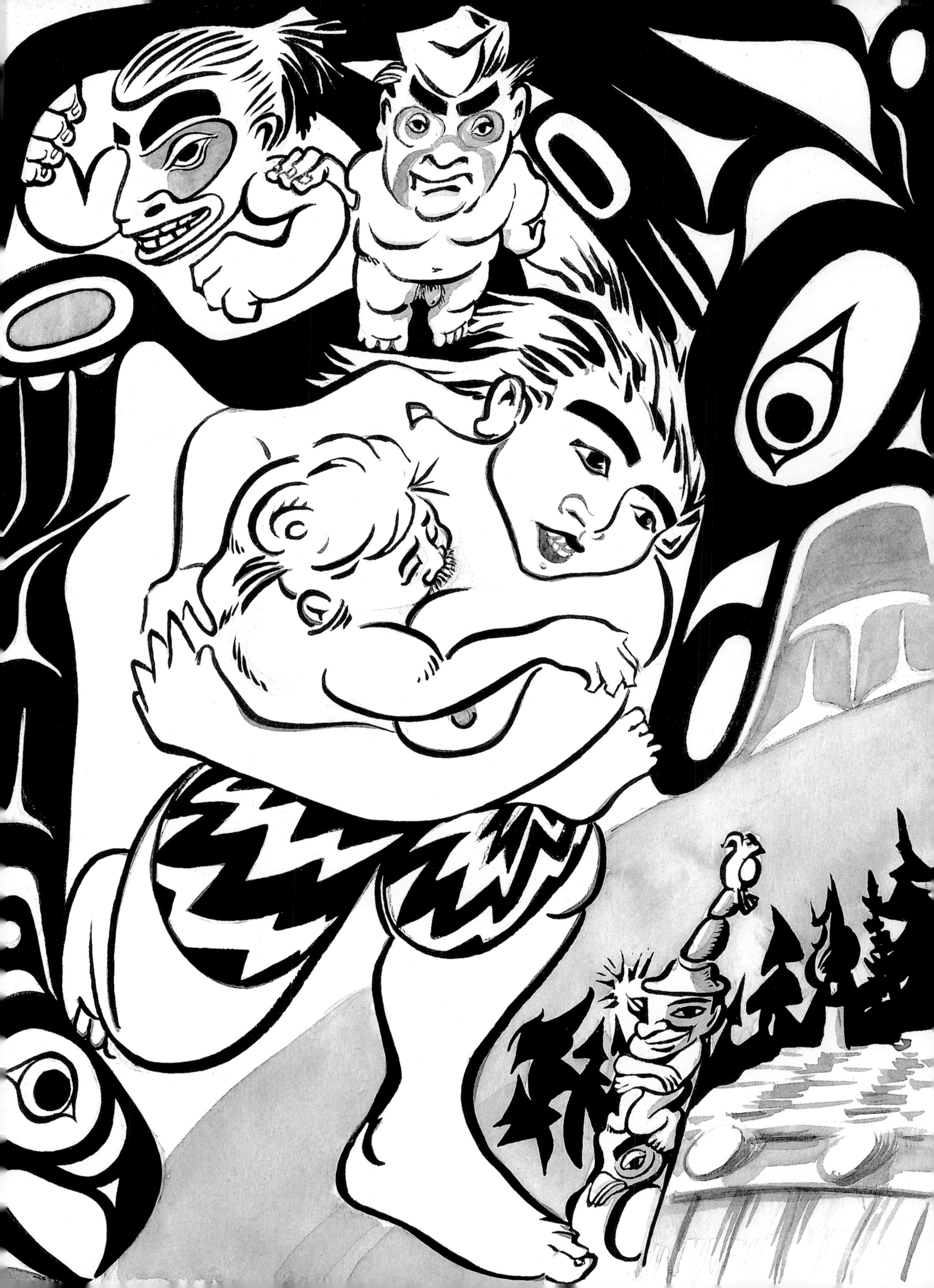

She placed the skin into his hands,
and his friend came back to life.

OM: "T'alang 'waadluuwaan.uu dang.ii suusaang," hin 'laa 'la
suudaayaan.

S: "Dang gud id 'waadluxan kihlgula g̱as ga," 'la gii 'la suu gan.

K: "T'aláng 'wáadluwaan uu dáng íi súusaang," hín 'láa 'll súudaayaan.

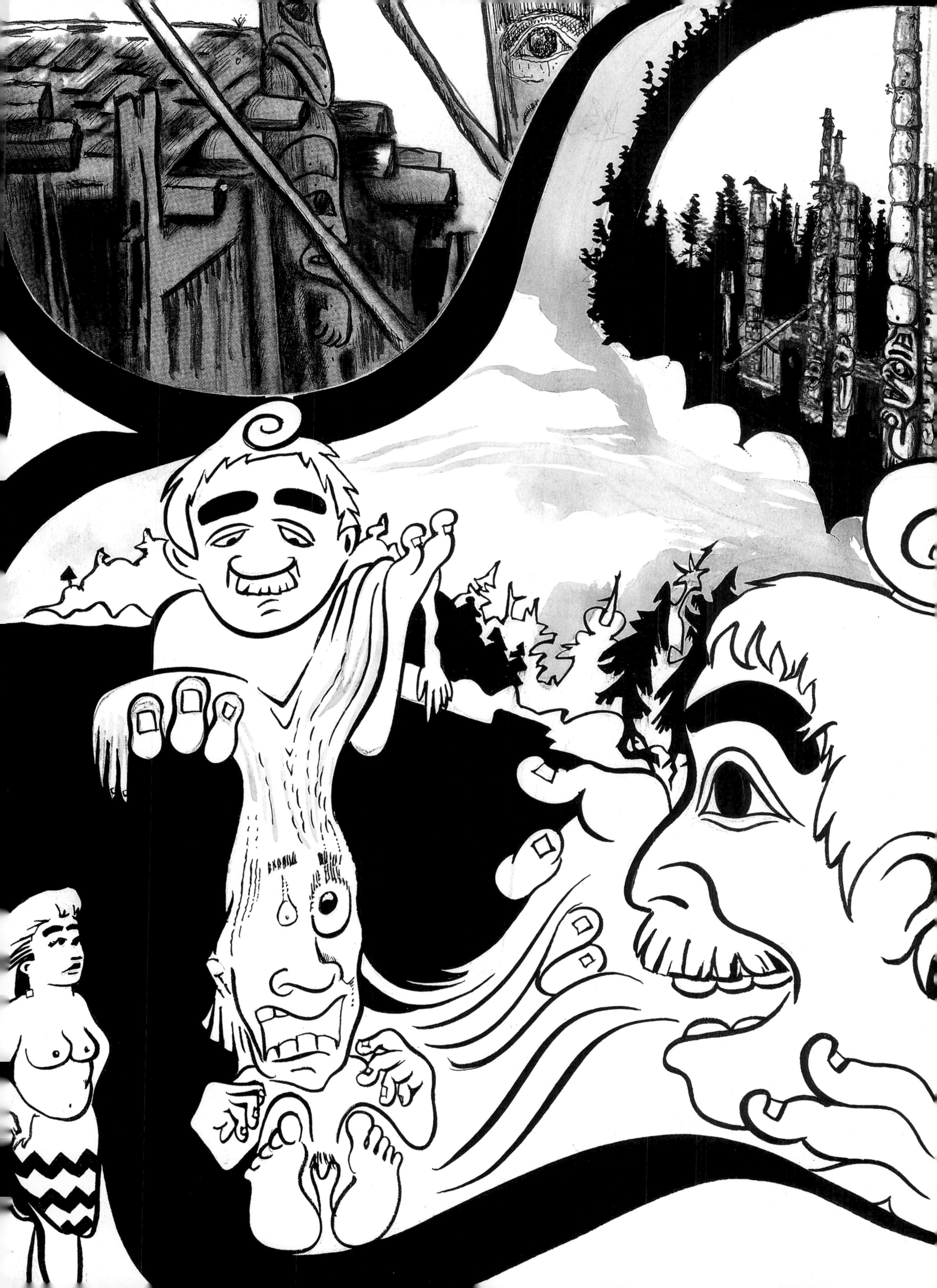

OM: ’Waa ginaan tl’a ’waadluwaan ’lee.ee suuidaan.
Hu tlaan G̲iiydang.

All that Spirit Dangerous to Offend said came to be.

S: Gen, tl’l ’waadlux̲an gud ’la kihlgul xidii.
Huu tlaan.

K: ’Wáa gingáan tl’ä ’wáadluwaan ’lée’ii súuïdaan.
Húu tláan G̲íidang.

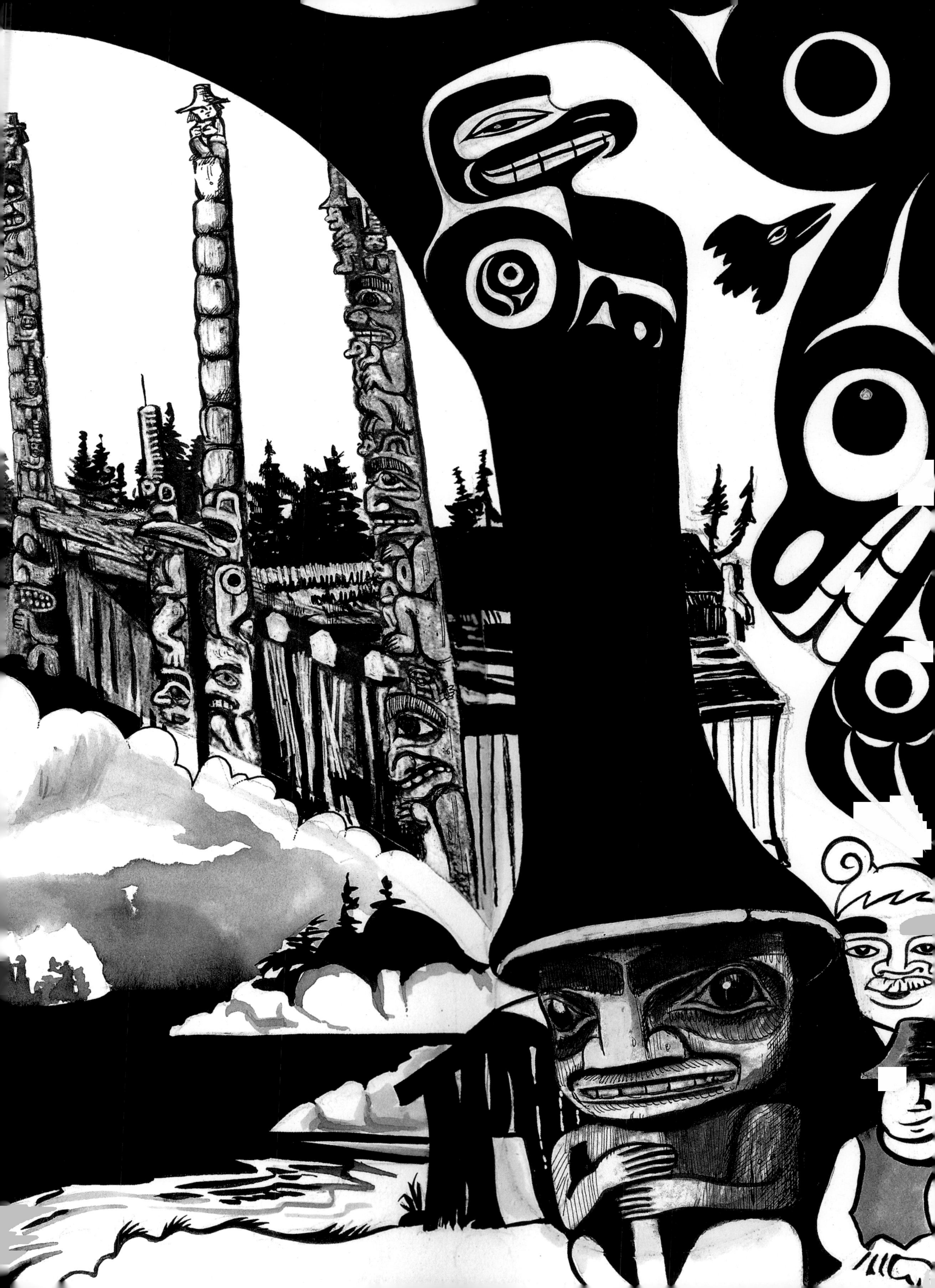

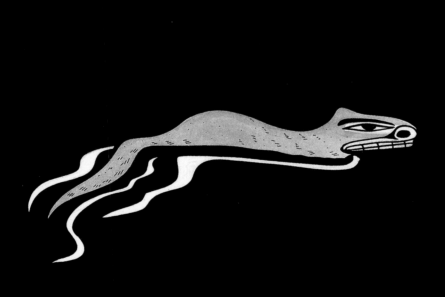

And that is all

A Note on Sources

The primary source for this ancient story is the 1908 edition of *Haida Texts: Masset Dialects* by John R. Swanton, published by E. J. Brill, Leiden, and G. E. Stechert, New York, v. 14, pt. 2 of the Memoirs of the American Museum of Natural History, and as v. 10, pt. 2 of the Publications of the Jesup North Pacific Expedition. Swanton, a 27-year-old linguist from Maine, transcribed the story told him by Kingagwo, Walter Kingagwaaw, of the Ghaw Sttlan Llnagaay of Yan. Here is the full English text:

A shaman at sk'a.aaws town had a partner.

They lived together, they loved each other very much.

"Let's leave" he said to his partner then.

"Where to?" he said to him. "To hlGaawt'a Point" he said to him.

And they left. Then the other shaman went ahead of him by canoe.

Then he saw a river otter swimming along. And he speared it.

And he killed it. Then he landed at the place they were moving to.

His partner, however, arrived after him.

Then he saw the otter that he [Shaman 2] had killed.

"Partner, you killed an otter, hey?" He said to him.

"Yes." He replied.

Then they worked at building their shack.

It was finished. They made a fire [inside it].

After they had eaten, he skinned his otter.

And he crammed a cedar [stretching] board in it. His partner was very happy with his skin.

And his [otter skin] got dry. then he pulled the board out of it.

He did this inside in the evening. The he wanted to turn its fur outward.

He started to try to turn it inside out.

His partner kept noticing that he was unable to do it.

"What are you going to make out of it?" he said to him.

"A beating stick case," he replied.

"Partner, give your [skin] here." He said [that] to him because
he was unable to fix it.

And he handed it to him across the fire.

The he [shaman 1] picked it up and turned with it to the wall.

He didn't turn it inside out. He fooled him.

He merely urinated into his [skin].

He didn't know that [the spirit of] the otter's skin went up
into his insides.

As soon as he handed the skin back to him [to its owner], his belly
began to ache.

"This is happening to you because you asked me for the otter,"
he [shaman 2] said to him.

"You speak the truth," he said to him.

He [shaman 1] died while he had not yet been sick for three days.

Then his partner used to cry hard.

Then they chopped off pieced [boards] of cedar for him.

"Build this [burial] for him up [on supporting columns] at the point,"
someone said.

It was his partner who said that. So they did.

Meanwhile his partner kept crying.

Then they put him in there [the burial structure], when it was ready.

It was quite far above the ground.

And they put him up on there [platform].

Then they made the roof of this [structure] watertight.

"When I die, have my head pointing this way," he said.

Just so they had his head lying in that direction.

His partner lived near him [the dead shaman.]

He would go to him and sit leaning again this [burial structure] of his and cry.

"I wonder why he asked me for the otter," he would say.

He finished crying and he left. And his wife used to fix food for him.

The day after that he went to him again as before.

Then he cried as before.

All the time he would blame himself. "I wonder why he asked me
for the otter," he would say.

After he had cried, he would sit there. Then evening came, while he was
sitting there.

Then a canoe with a crew of four rapidly approached where he lived.

The person in the middle wore a big hat. He was a big shaman.

"Land below the shaman on the platform by the trees," he said.

"Get off and go to him," he [the big shaman] said to the one in the bow.

Accordingly he went up to him. They did not see his partner
sitting below him.

Then this one who got off, he kept wiggling the head of this dead person back and forth.

His partner was watching that. And he pulled off his skin.

Then he went down to the water with it.

And his partner too stayed with his partner's skin, when they put his [skin] aboard.

This big shaman, he used to go around looking for the skins of shamans, of dead ones, that is.

There were many of their skins that he had put aboard the canoe.

No one saw him get aboard the canoe behind this big shaman.

Then he [shaman 2] pushed his knees against him hard.

Then his [back]started to ache very much where his knees were against it.

After he had ached for a while, he would slide away from him on his bum again.

"Take me right away," he [the big shaman] kept on saying.

Then they landed with him.

And they put the many shamans' skins aboard the canoe in the house.

Then this big shaman went into his own house.

And they took up [to the house] his partner's skin and he went up with it.

There was a rail-like thing stretching all the way around the inside of the house.

That was full of them [shaman's skins]

This is what he [the big shaman]had been doing for some time.

"Have that one hang over there," he heard them say of his partner's skin.

Just so they hung his apart from the rest.

Then he [the big shaman] sat down again.

The when he grabbed his waist again, he pushed his knees hard
against his back as before.

Then he ached badly as before.

Then they went to hire a shaman.

He kept performing around him hard.

After he had ached a while, he would move him over away from himself.

He continually sat behind him.

This shaman failed to save him.

They went again to hire someone else.

They landed at his [the big shaman's] place with that one too.

That one too performed around him continually.

And he too failed with him.

They hired ten shamans for him.

All that time he held him against himself.

When the spirits [they hired] came to ten, they gave up hope.

They went to get spirit Dangerous to Offend.

Then they landed with him.

While he was still going along some distance away on the canoe, he saw this
shaman sitting behind this [big] shaman.

Because he had taken his partner's skin, he gave him an intolerable ailment.

When this shaman landed, he went inside.

Then he saw him sitting behind him.

"When I come in, don't embarrass me," he said to him.

"Then I will speak through you," he said.

Therefore, he left him alone. And he was saved.

Just so, he began to speak through him.

And Spirit Dangerous to Offend went back.

He had many clanspeople.

Then just as he had promised to speak through this shaman,
he spoke through him.

"We will all speak through you," he told him.

Just so, they all began to speak through him.

That is all.

Acknowledgements

To create three living versions of the story recorded by Swanton, the text was translated into modern orthography by Old Massett dialect scholar Jaskwaan, Amanda Bedard, guided by her language training with Elders 'Ills gidee, Primrose Adams; Nang K'alaagaa, June Russ; Gulkihlgad, Dr. Marianne Ignace; and the late Sk'adada 'Leeyga, Stephen Brown. This updated text was then translated into the Skidegate dialect by the Elders at HlGaagilda Xaayda Kil Naay (Skidegate Haida Immersion Program or SHIP): K'inwas, Winnifred Casey; ILdagwaay, Bea Harley; Gaayinguuhlas, Roy Jones Sr.; Yang K'aalas, Grace Jones; Taalgyaa'adad, Betty Richardson; Jiixa, Gladys Vandal; SGaanajaadsk'yaagaxiigangs, Kathleen Hans; Sing.giduu, Laura Jormanainen; and Niis Waan, Harvey Williams, working with Jisgang, Nika Collison, Haida Gwaii Museum at Kay Llnagaay; and into the Kaigani or K'íis Xaadee (Alaskan Haida) dialect by K'uyáang, Benjamin Young, who would like to acknowledge the support of Skíl Jáadei, Linda Schrack, and Ilskyalas, Delores Churchill, as well as every Elder who contributed to the creation of the Alaskan Haida Dictionary under the guidance of Jordan Lachler, including Kúng Skiís, Claude Morrison; Áljuhl, Erma Lawrence; Dlaadaay, Woodrow Morrison; and Yátch Géi, Anna Peele.

The English version of the story has a much simpler origin story; I read and absorbed the three versions I mentioned in the foreword and then retold it in a way that made the most sense to me. Stories can be told in many different ways. Some are recognizable as myth, history and parable. And like everything else in this amazing world, they change. What doesn't change is how stories must serve a purpose for the living. A story without purpose vanishes. This story has not vanished. Even though it was scattered and separated like ourselves during these hard times of terrible troubles it is still here. Therefore it has a purpose.

My small contribution to you, the living champions of language, is to pull a brush across a story that ask us all to see, to love and, perhaps most importantly of all, to not be invisible.

Playfully,
MNY

This edition published in 2018 by Locarno Press
4510 West 4th Avenue, Vancouver BC Canada V6R1R3
locarnopress.com

First edition published in 2000 by Theytus Books
and the Haida Gwaii Museum

CIP data is available from Library and Archives Canada
ISBN 978-1-988996-00-4

We gratefully acknowledge for their financial support of our publishing program the Canada Council for the Arts, the BC Arts Council, and the Government of Canada through the Canada Book Fund (CBF).

Printed in Malaysia

10 9 8 7 6 5 4 3 2 1

Cover and interior design by Naomi MacDougall
Edited by Scott Steedman

Canada Council for the Arts Conseil des arts du Canada

Canada

British Columbia | British Columbia Arts Council

MICHAEL NICOLL YAHGULANAAS is the creator of Haida Manga, a distinctive fusion of pop graphics, Haida art and Japanese comic styles. His books include *A Tale of Two Shamans*; *Flight of the Hummingbird*; *Hachidori*, a bestseller in Japan; *Red*, nominated for a BC Book Award, a Doug Wright Award for Best Book, and a 2010 Joe Shuster Award for Outstanding Canadian Cartoonist, and an Amazon Top 100 book of 2009; and *War of the Blink*.

Yahgulanaas is also a sculptor and graphic artist whose work is in the collections of the British Museum, Metropolitan Museum of Art, Seattle Art Museum, Vancouver Art Gallery, Vancouver International Airport, City of Vancouver, City of Kamloops and University of British Columbia. He pulls from his 20 years of political experience in the Council of the Haida Nation and continues to work as an activated artist with progressive businesses, institutions and communities about social justice, community building, communication and change management. In 2015, he was named the first ever Artist-in-Residence at the American Museum of Natural History in New York.

Yahgulanaas lives on an island in the Salish Sea, with his wife and daughter.